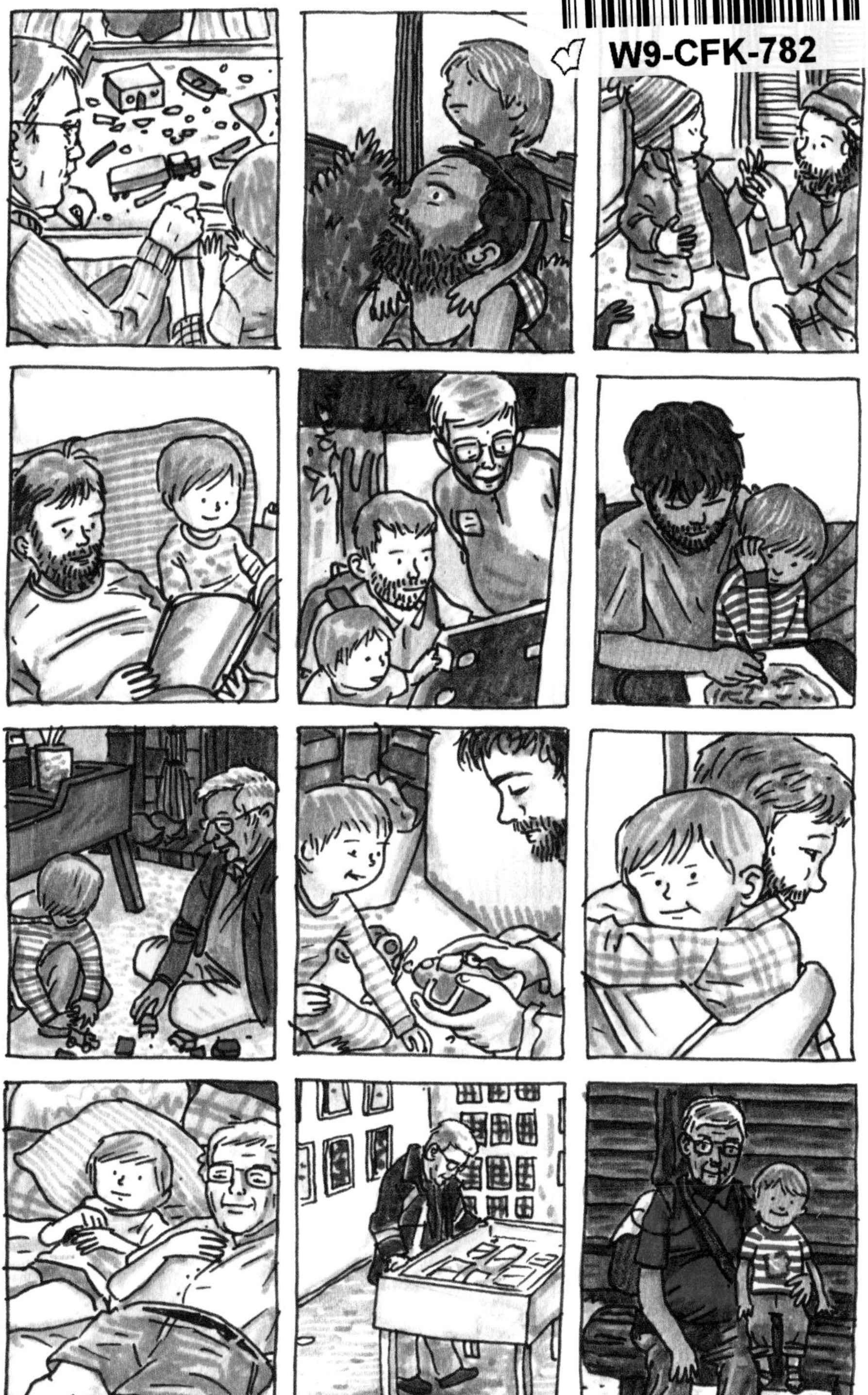

A MATTER OF LIFE

BY JEFFREY BROWN

TOP SHELF PRODUCTIONS

CHICAGO · ATLANTA · PORTLAND · NEW YORK

Published by Top Shelf Productions
P.O. Box 1282
Marietta GA 30061-1282
USA

Publishers: Brett Warnock + Chris Staros

Visit our online catalog at: www.topshelfcomix.com

First printing: July 2013.
9 8 7 6 5 4 3 2 1
Printed in China.

ISBN 978-1-60309-266-1

Although this book is essentially autobiographical, it should not be viewed as a necessarily true or accurate portrayal of any of the events depicted, nor of any of the people within or their character. The contents of this book are based on the feelings and memories of the author, and should not be considered to represent the viewpoint of any other person.

"Not If, But When" originally appeared in a different form as part of the Creative Time Comics series.

For Dad
and Oscar

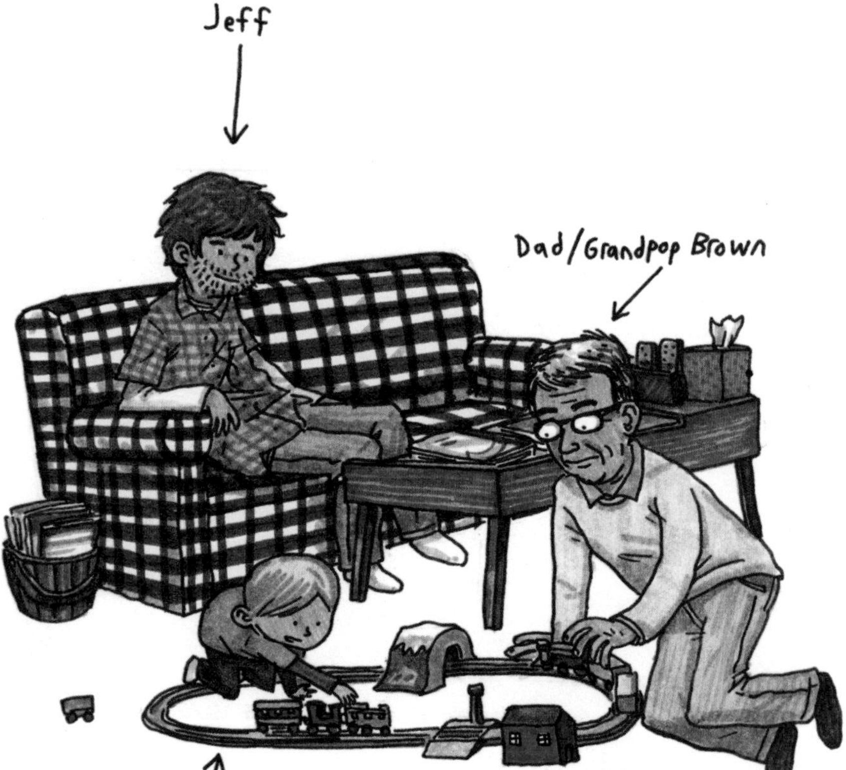
Jeff
Dad/Grandpop Brown
Oscar

A
MATTER
OF
LIFE

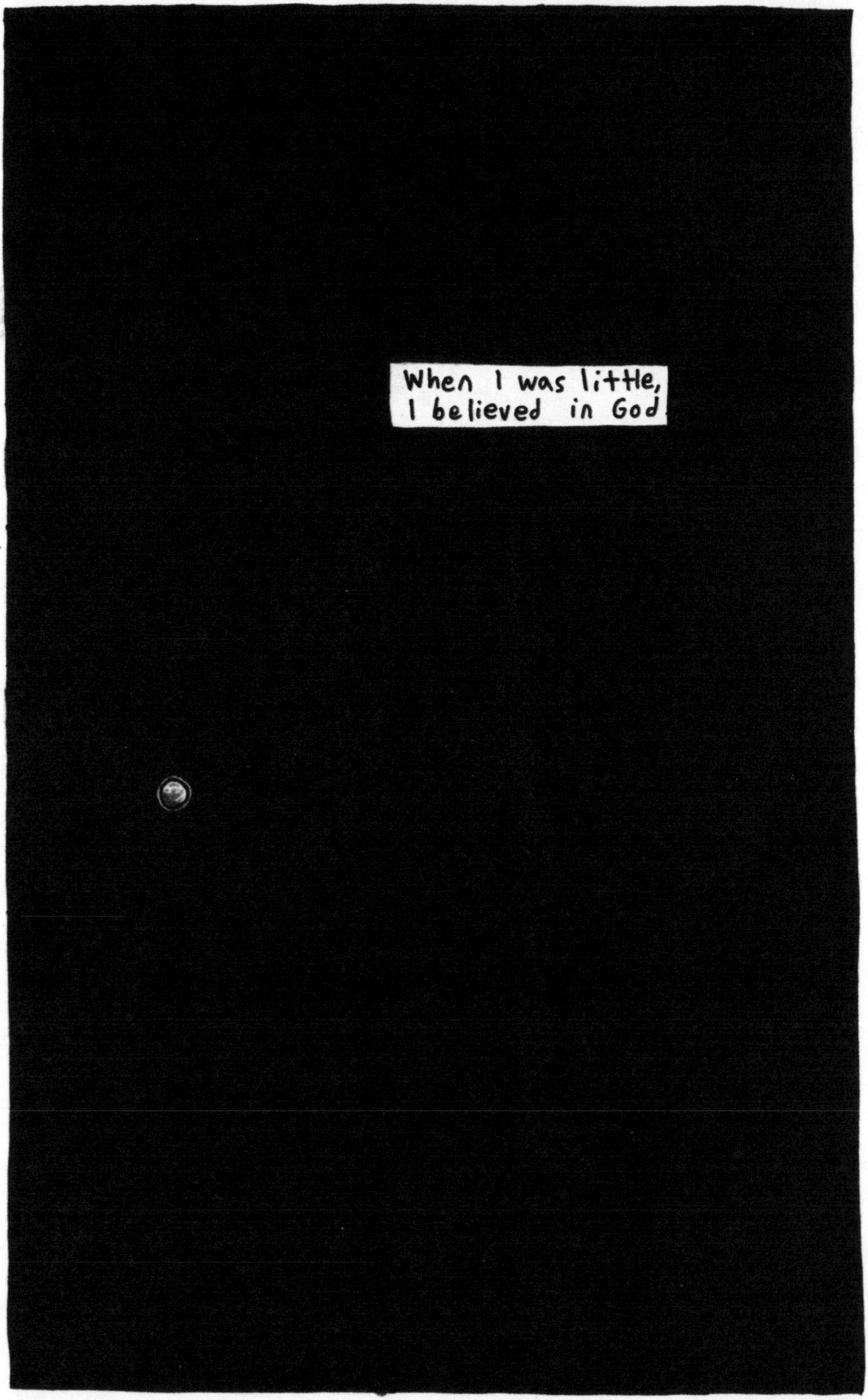
When I was little, I believed in God.

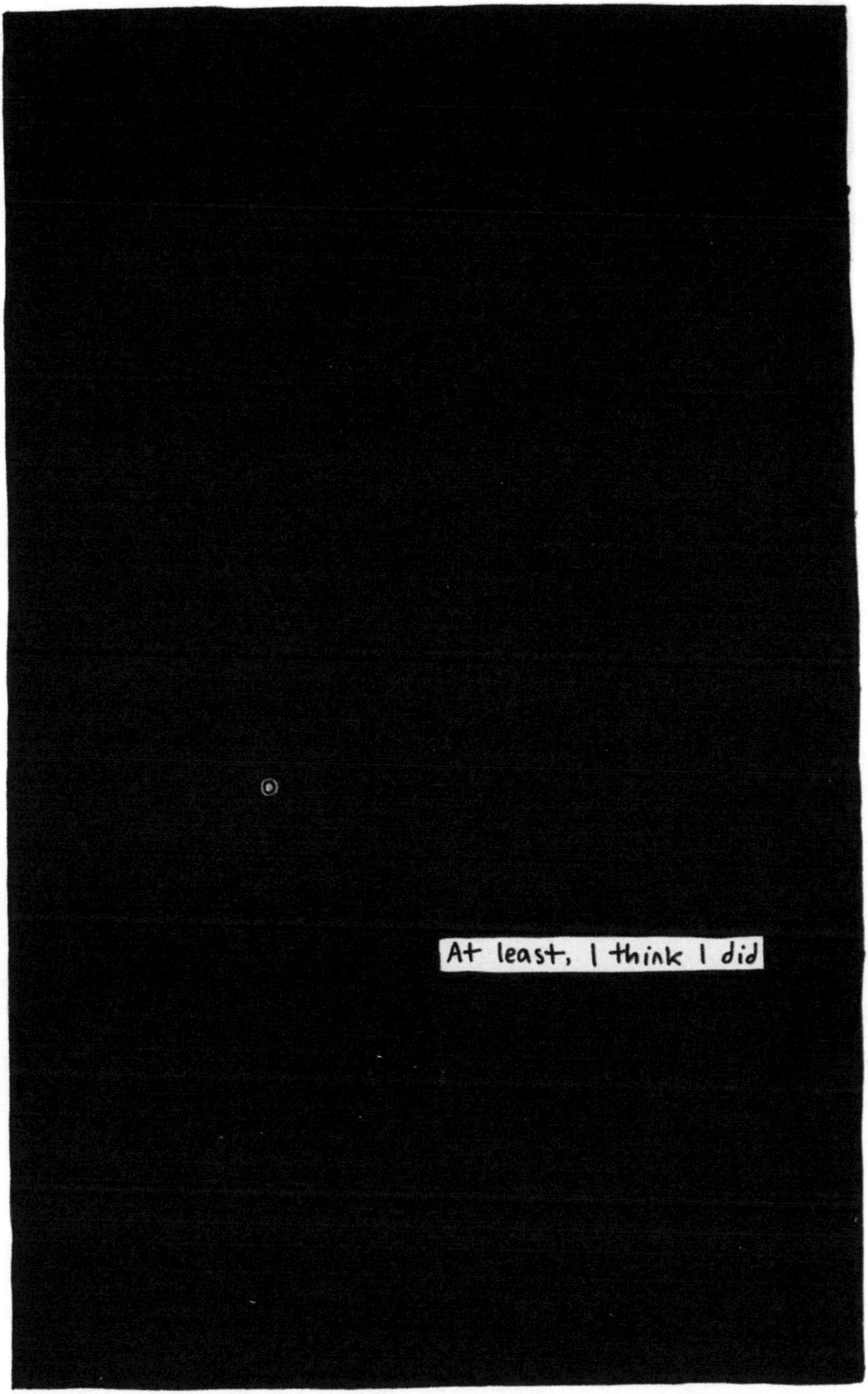

At least, I think I did

7

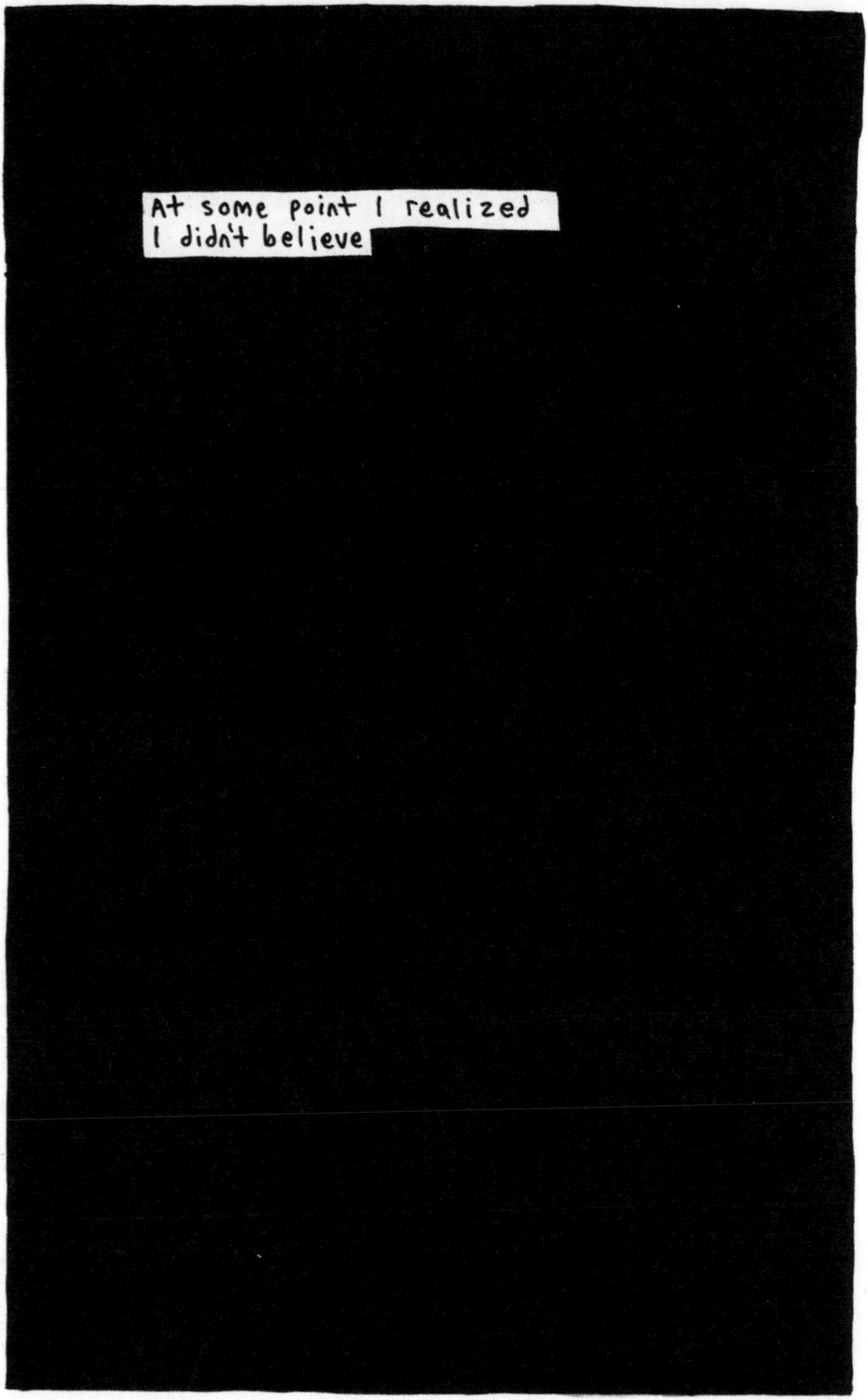
At some point I realized
I didn't believe

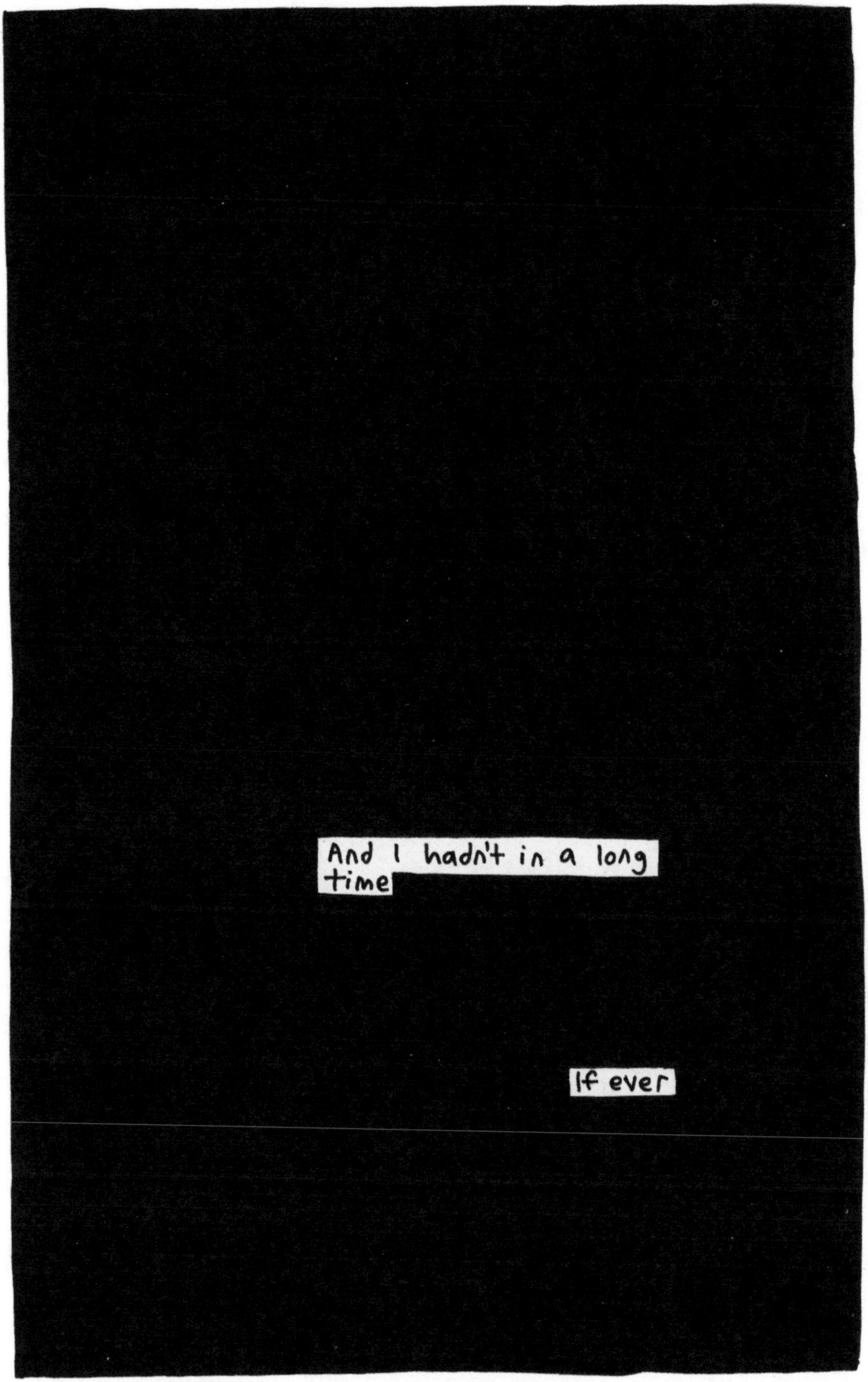
And I hadn't in a long time
If ever

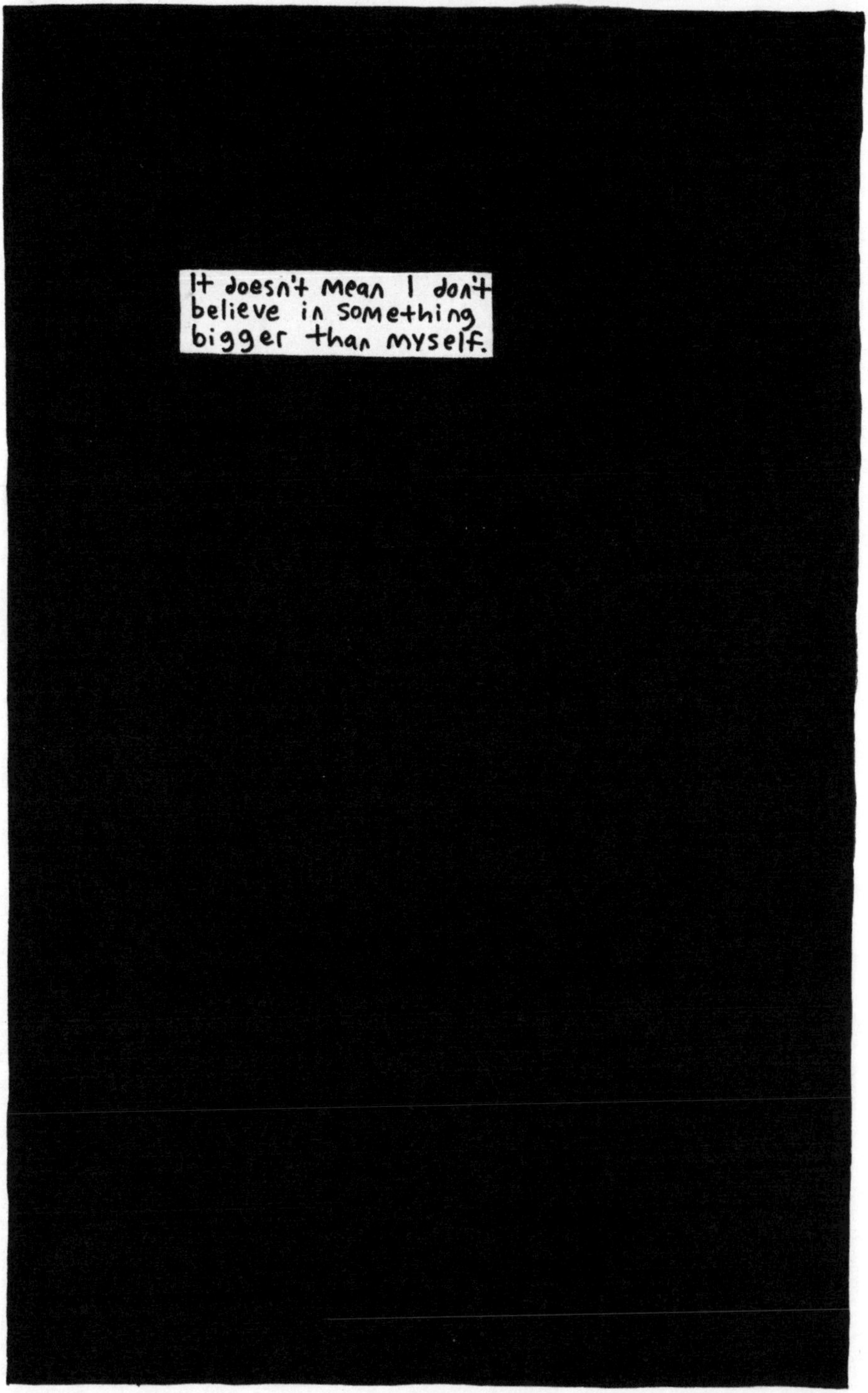
It doesn't mean I don't believe in something bigger than myself.

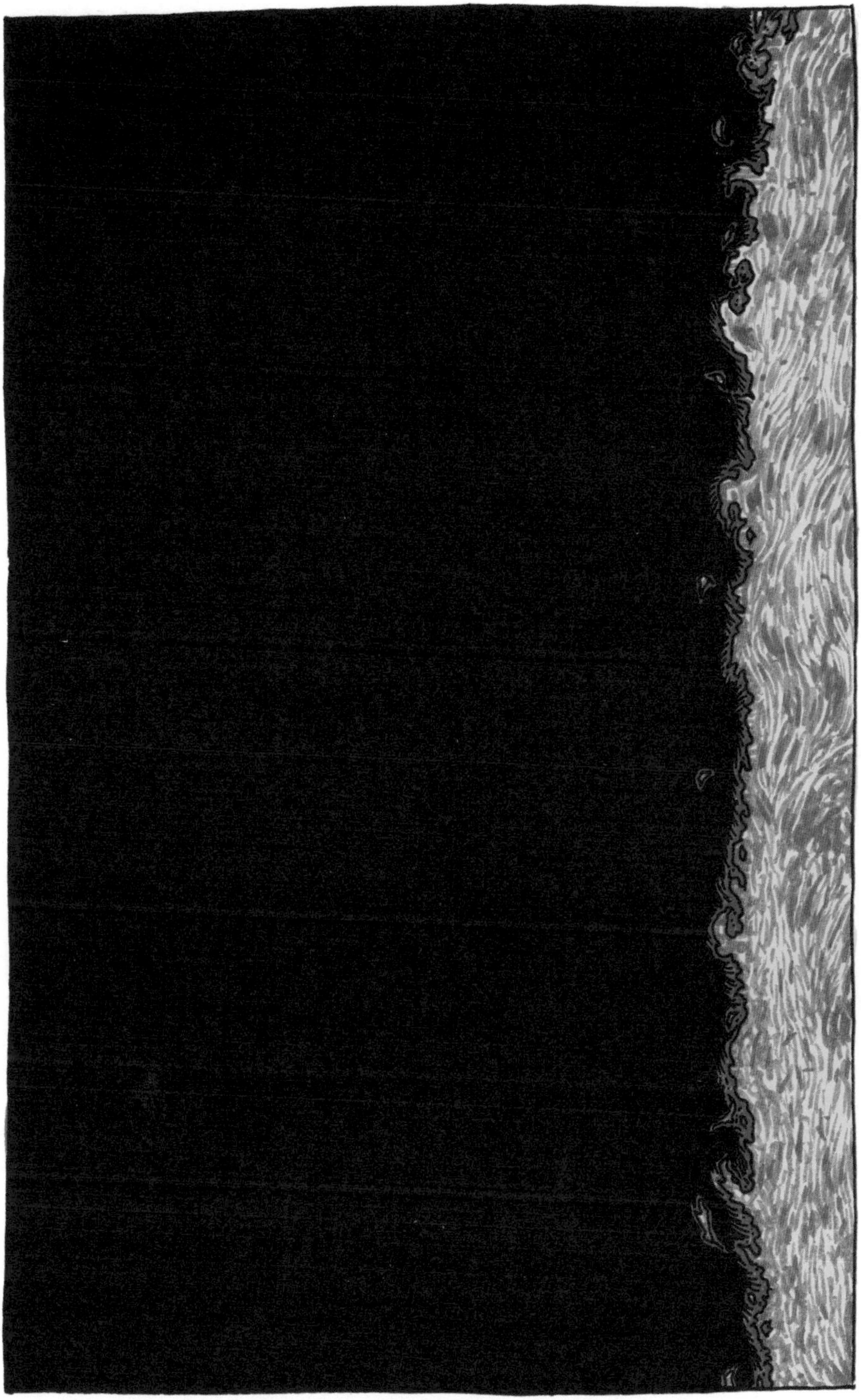

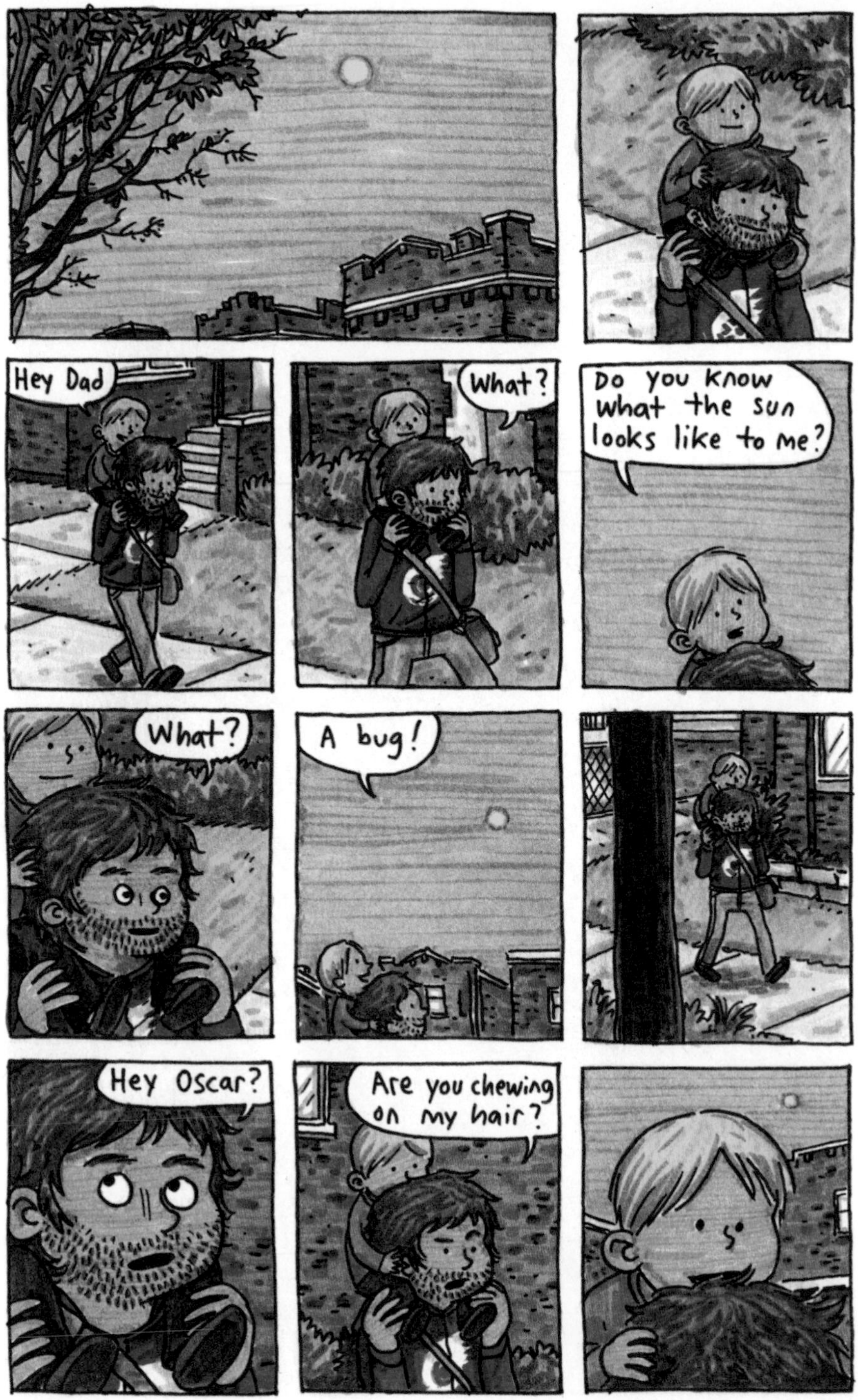
Hey Dad
What?
Do you know what the sun looks like to me?
What?
A bug!
Hey Oscar?
Are you chewing on my hair?

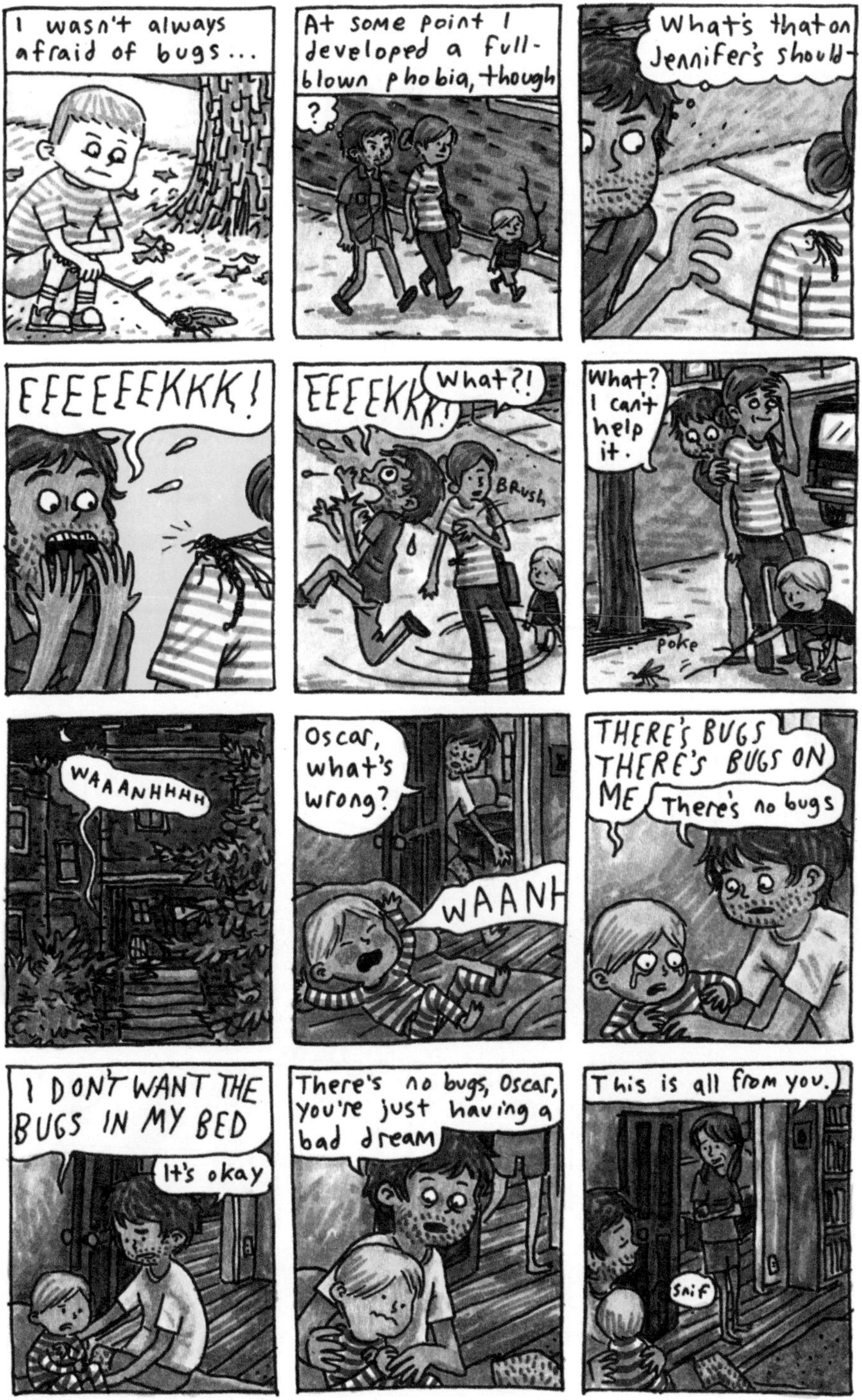
I wasn't always afraid of bugs...
At some point I developed a full-blown phobia, though
?
What's that on Jennifer's should-
EEEEEEKKK!
EEEEKKK!
What?!
BRUSH
What? I can't help it.
poke
WAAANHHHH
Oscar, what's wrong?
WAANH
THERE'S BUGS THERE'S BUGS ON ME
There's no bugs
I DON'T WANT THE BUGS IN MY BED
It's okay
There's no bugs, Oscar, you're just having a bad dream
This is all from you.
snif

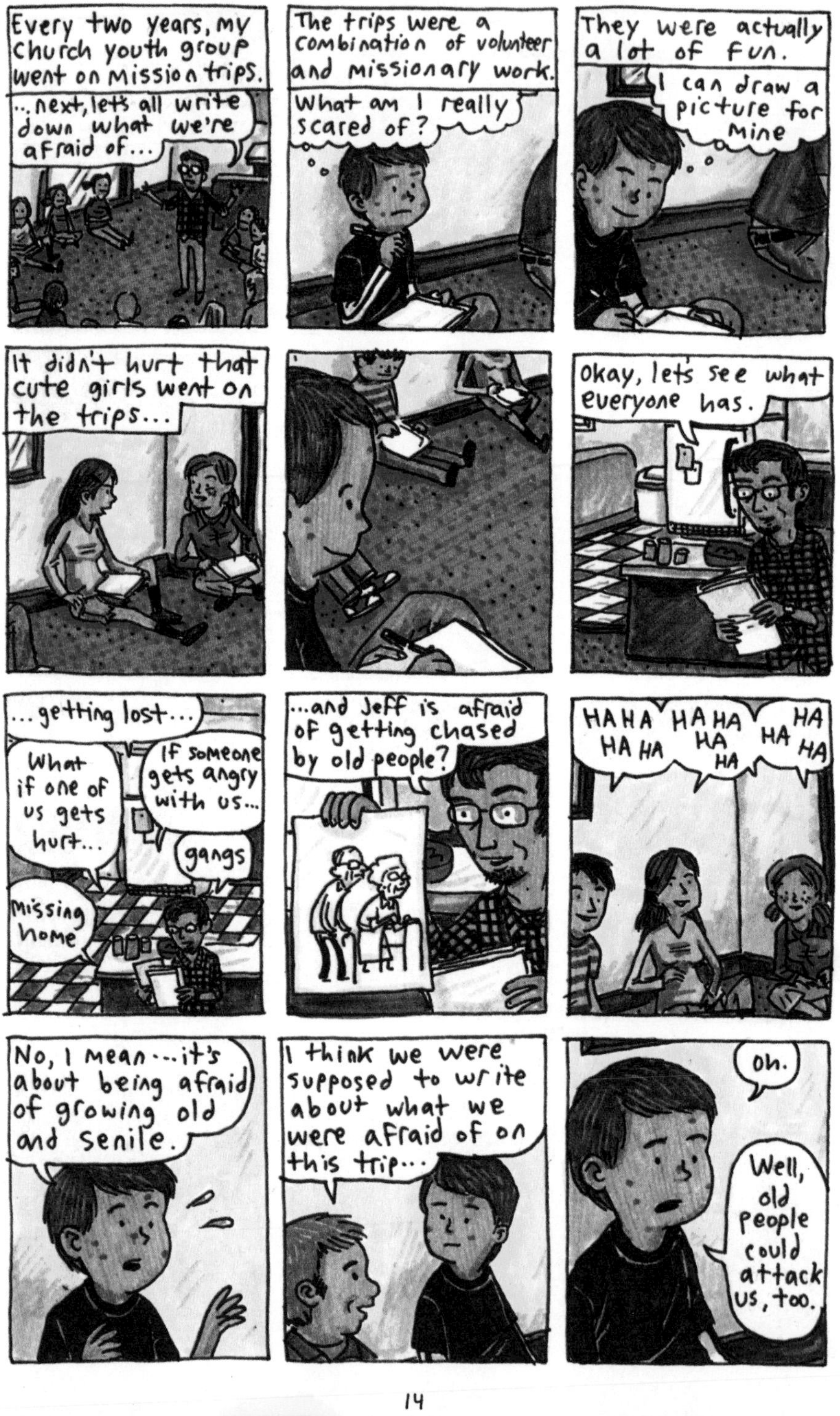
Every two years, my church youth group went on mission trips.
...next, let's all write down what we're afraid of...
The trips were a combination of volunteer and missionary work.
What am I really scared of?
They were actually a lot of fun.
I can draw a picture for mine
It didn't hurt that cute girls went on the trips...
Okay, let's see what everyone has.
...getting lost...
What if one of us gets hurt...
If someone gets angry with us...
gangs
Missing home
...and Jeff is afraid of getting chased by old people?
HAHA HAHA
HAHA HA HA
HA HA HA HA
No, I mean...it's about being afraid of growing old and senile.
I think we were supposed to write about what we were afraid of on this trip...
Oh.
Well, old people could attack us, too.

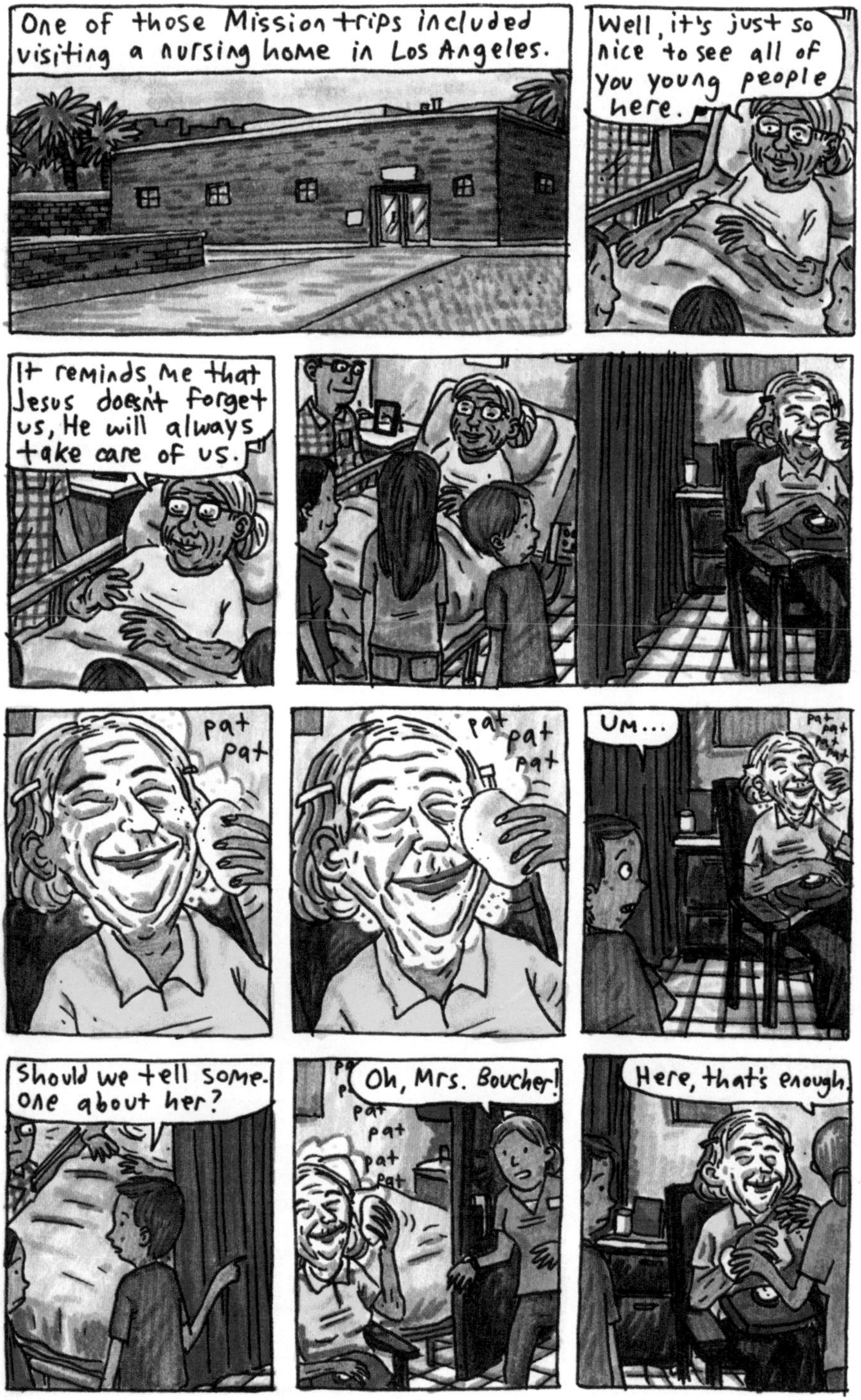
One of those Mission trips included visiting a nursing home in Los Angeles.
Well, it's just so nice to see all of you young people here.
It reminds me that Jesus doesn't forget us, He will always take care of us.
pat pat
pat pat pat
Um...
Should we tell someone about her?
pat pat pat pat
Oh, Mrs. Boucher!
Here, that's enough.

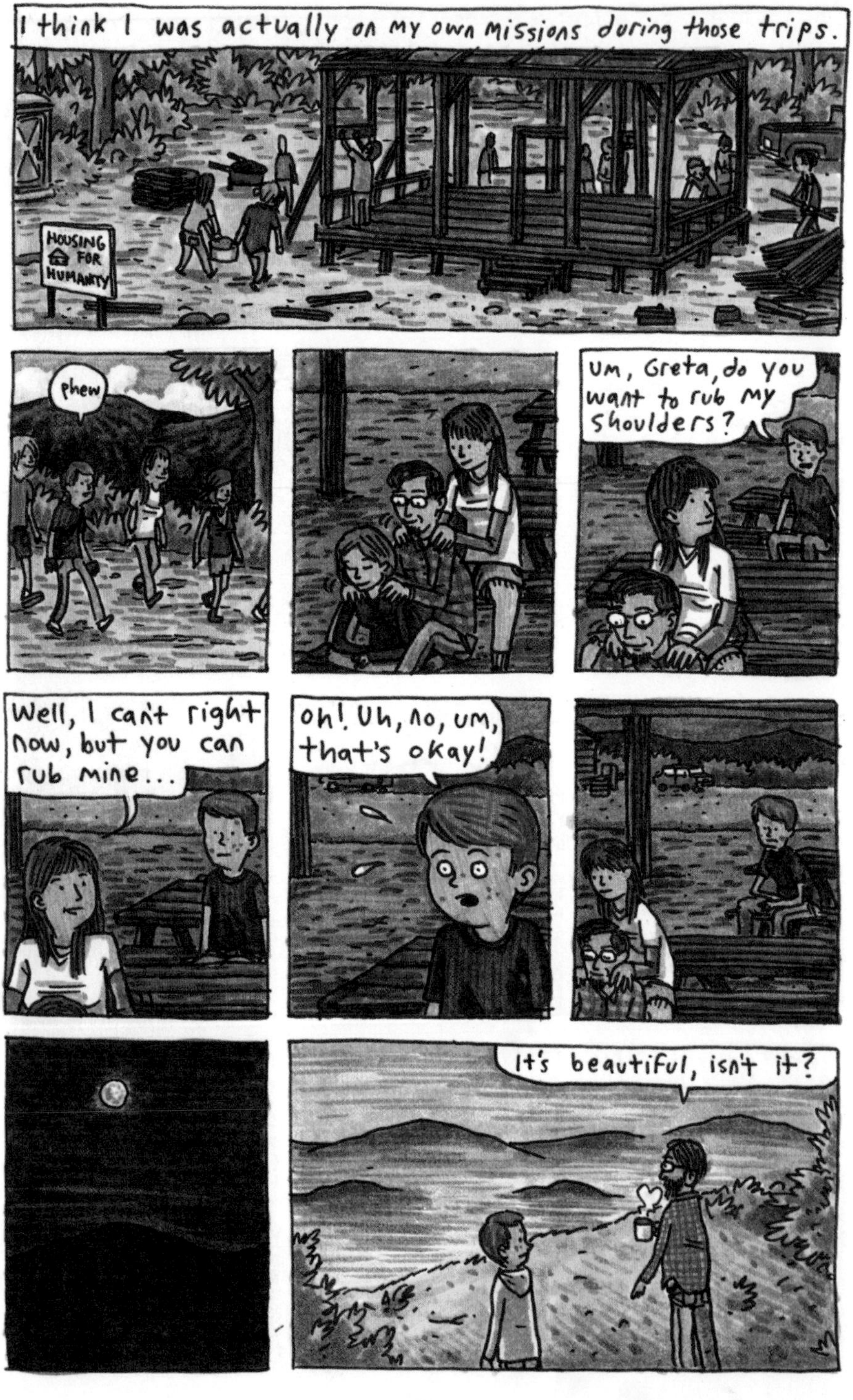
I think I was actually on my own missions during those trips.
HOUSING FOR HUMANITY
phew
Um, Greta, do you want to rub my shoulders?
Well, I can't right now, but you can rub mine...
Oh! Uh, no, um, that's okay!
It's beautiful, isn't it?

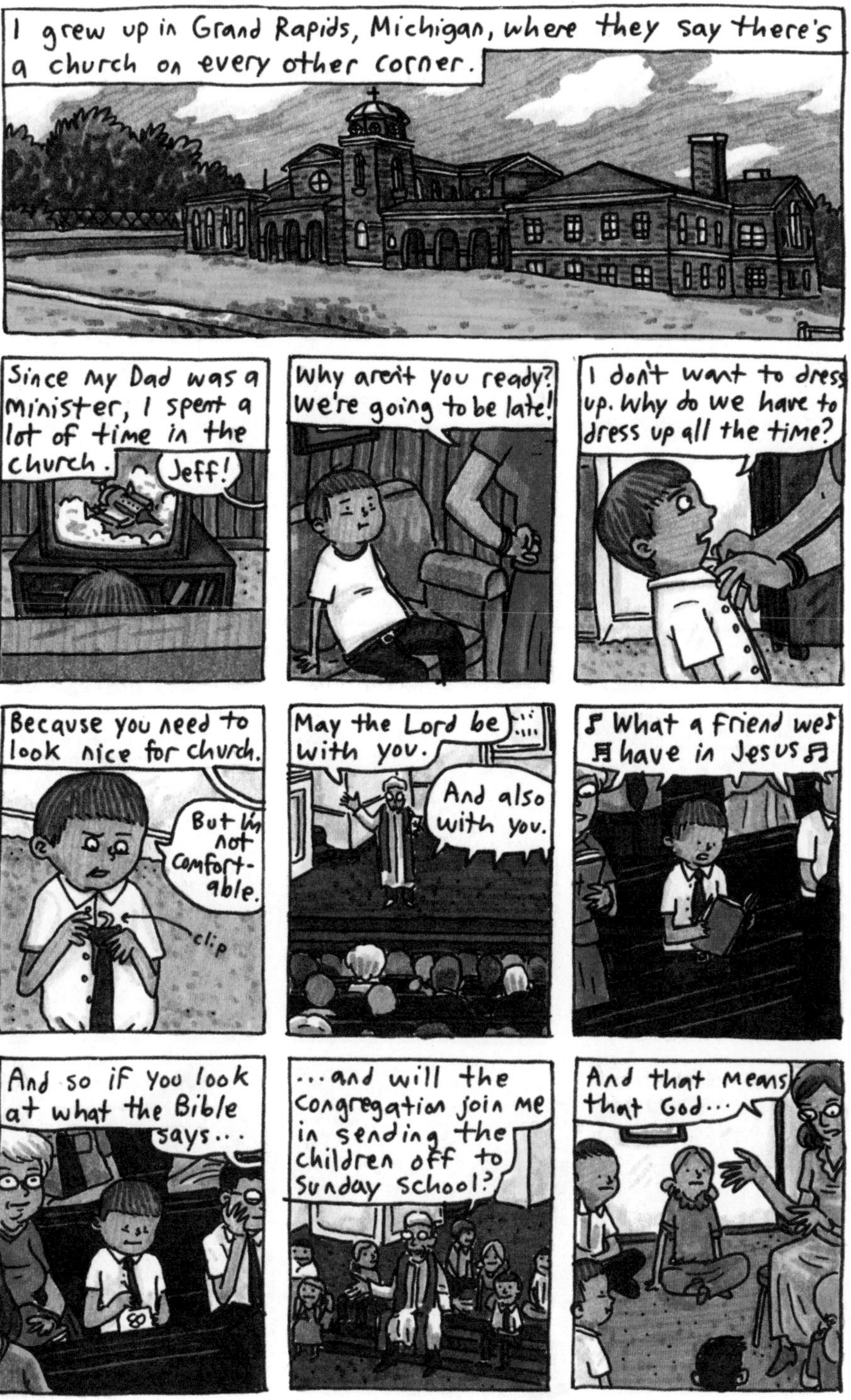
I grew up in Grand Rapids, Michigan, where they say there's a church on every other corner.
Since my Dad was a minister, I spent a lot of time in the church.
Jeff!
Why aren't you ready? We're going to be late!
I don't want to dress up. Why do we have to dress up all the time?
Because you need to look nice for church.
But I'm not comfortable.
clip
May the Lord be with you.
And also with you.
What a friend we have in Jesus
And so if you look at what the Bible says...
...and will the congregation join me in sending the children off to Sunday School?
And that means that God...

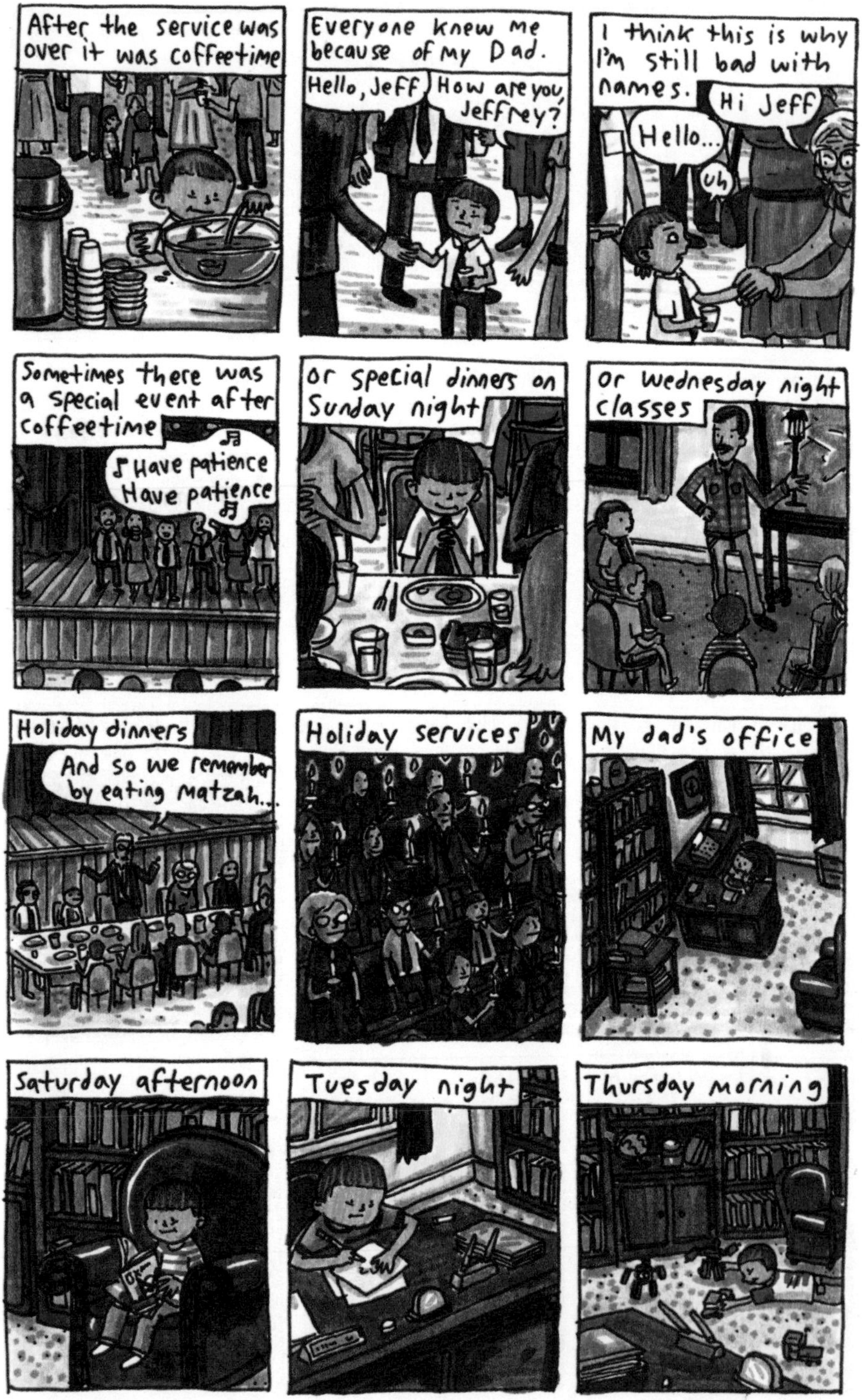
After the service was over it was coffeetime
Everyone knew me because of my Dad.
Hello, Jeff
How are you, Jeffrey?
I think this is why I'm still bad with names.
Hi Jeff
Hello...
uh
Sometimes there was a special event after coffeetime
Have patience Have patience
or special dinners on Sunday night
or Wednesday night classes
Holiday dinners
And so we remember by eating matzah...
Holiday services
My dad's office
Saturday afternoon
Tuesday night
Thursday morning

Today the fourth grade Sunday School class will recite from the Bible.

Please hold your applause until all the children have spoken.

I will recite Psalm 23. The Lord is my shepherd, I shall not want. He makes me lie down in green pastures...

...goodness and mercy shall follow me all the days of my life, and I shall dwell in the house of the Lord my whole life long.

phew!

I will recite the first five books of the Bible. Genesis, Exodus, Leviticus, Numbers, Deuteronomy.

CLAP CLAP

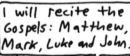

CLAP CLAP CLAP CLAP! CLAP CLAP CLAP! CLAP CLAP CLAP! CLAP CLAP CLAP!

I will recite the Gospels: Matthew, Mark, Luke and John.

CLAP CLAP CLAP! CLAP CLAP CLAP! CLAP CLAP CLAP! CLAP CLAP CLAP!

I will recite First Corinthians 13, verse 4. Love is patient, love is kind.

CLAP CLAP CLAP! CLAP CLAP CLAP! CLAP CLAP CLAP! CLAP CLAP CLAP CLAP!

They were supposed to wait to clap... now no one clapped for me!

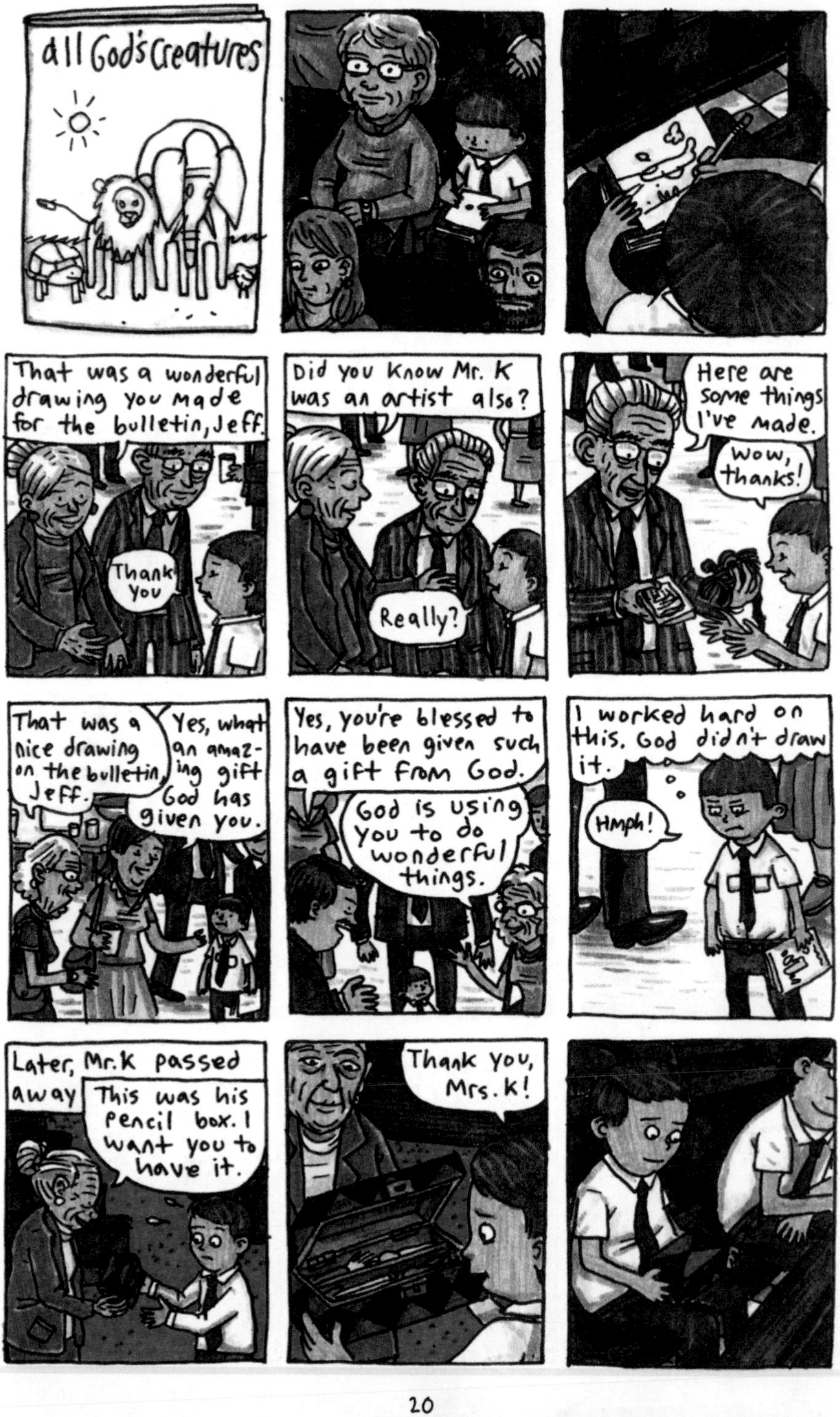
all God's creatures
That was a wonderful drawing you made for the bulletin, Jeff.
Thank you
Did you know Mr. K was an artist also?
Really?
Here are some things I've made.
Wow, thanks!
That was a nice drawing on the bulletin, Jeff.
Yes, what an amazing gift God has given you.
Yes, you're blessed to have been given such a gift from God.
God is using you to do wonderful things.
I worked hard on this. God didn't draw it.
Hmph!
Later, Mr. K passed away
This was his pencil box. I want you to have it.
Thank you, Mrs. K!

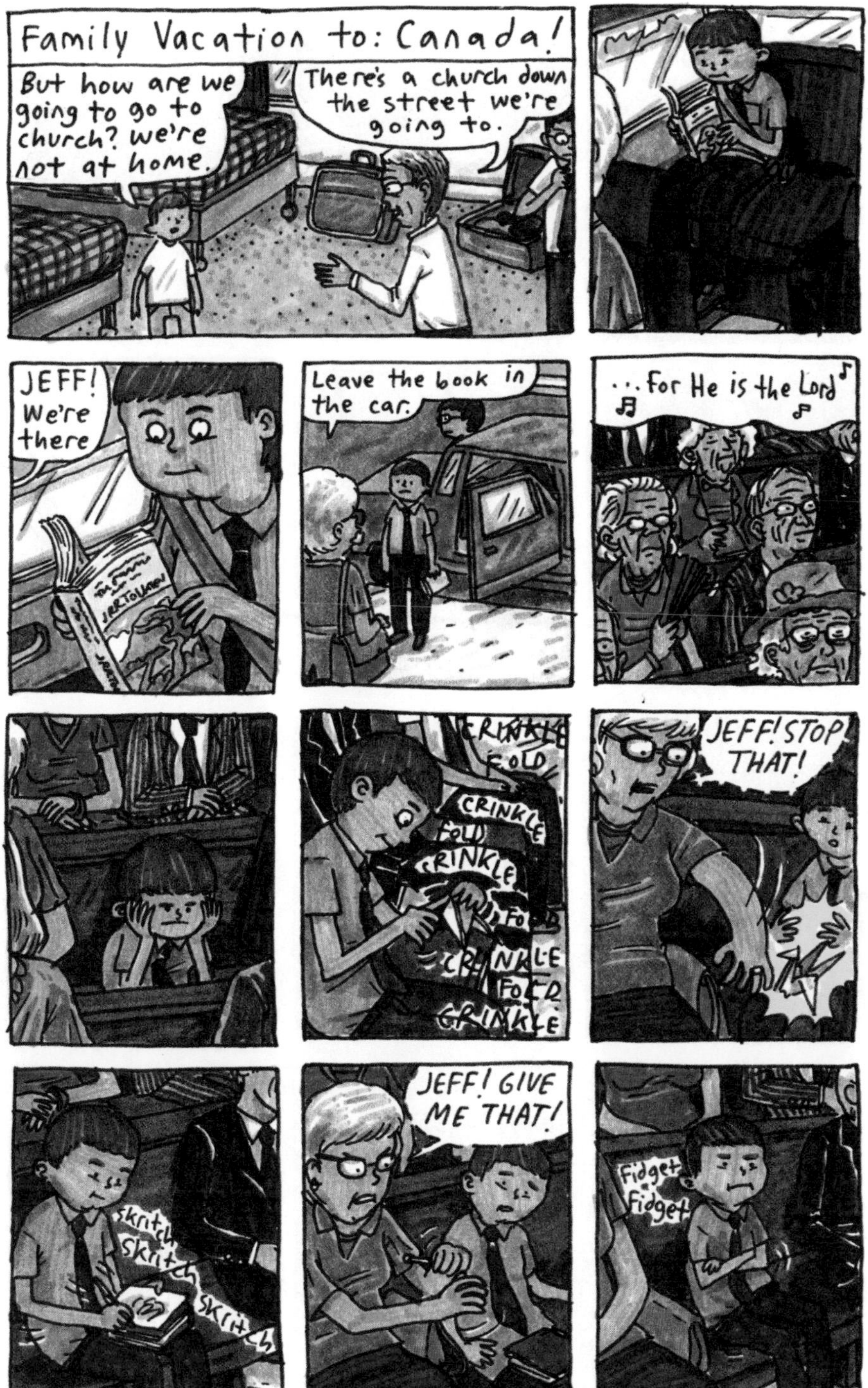
Family Vacation to: Canada!
But how are we going to go to church? we're not at home.
There's a church down the street we're going to.
JEFF! We're there
Leave the book in the car.
...For He is the Lord
CRINKLE
FOLD
CRINKLE
FOLD
CRINKLE
FOLD
CRINKLE
FOLD
CRINKLE
JEFF! STOP THAT!
skritch
skritch
skritch
JEFF! GIVE ME THAT!
Fidget
Fidget

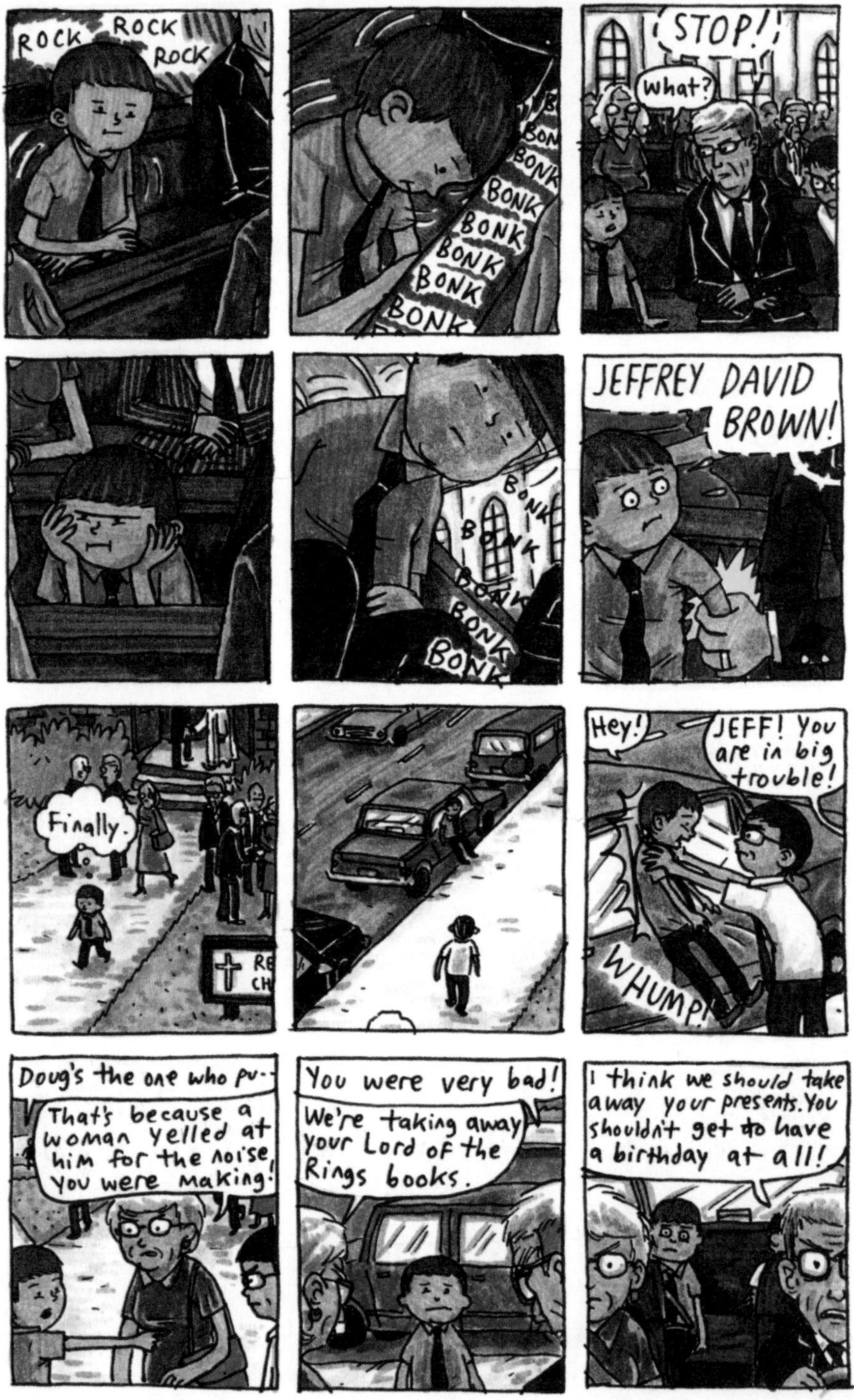

ROCK ROCK ROCK
BONK BONK BONK BONK BONK BONK BONK
STOP!
What?
BONK BONK BONK BONK BONK
JEFFREY DAVID BROWN!
Finally.
Hey!
JEFF! You are in big trouble!
WHUMP!
Doug's the one who pu--
That's because a woman yelled at him for the noise you were making!
You were very bad!
We're taking away your Lord of the Rings books.
I think we should take away your presents. You shouldn't get to have a birthday at all!

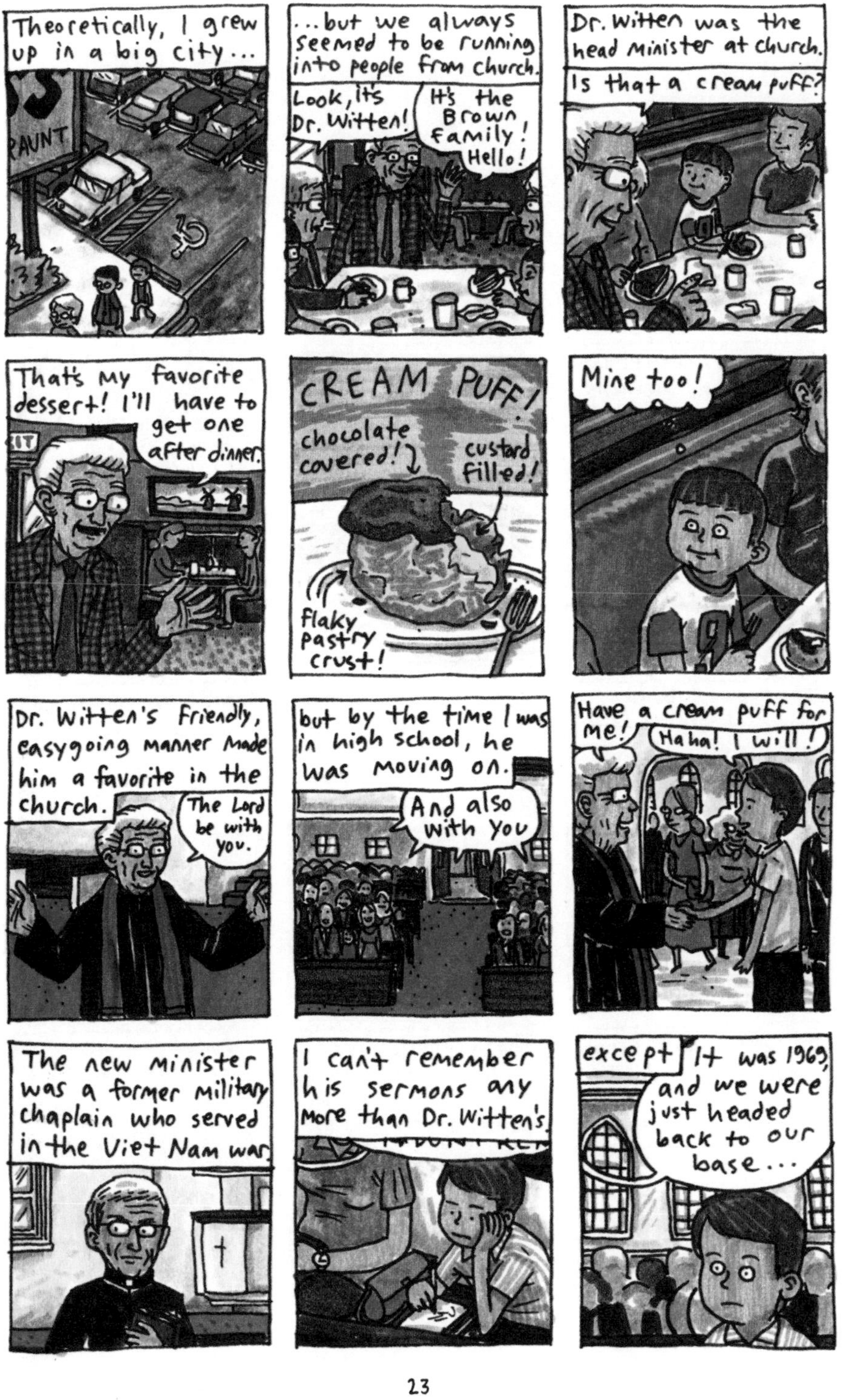
Theoretically, I grew up in a big city...
RAUNT
...but we always seemed to be running into people from church.
Look, it's Dr. Witten!
It's the Brown family! Hello!
Dr. Witten was the head minister at church.
Is that a cream puff?
That's my favorite dessert! I'll have to get one after dinner.
CREAM PUFF!
chocolate covered!
custard filled!
flaky pastry crust!
Mine too!
Dr. Witten's friendly, easygoing manner made him a favorite in the church.
The Lord be with you.
but by the time I was in high school, he was moving on.
And also with you
Have a cream puff for me!
Haha! I will!
The new minister was a former military chaplain who served in the Viet Nam war.
I can't remember his sermons any more than Dr. Witten's.
except
It was 1969, and we were just headed back to our base...

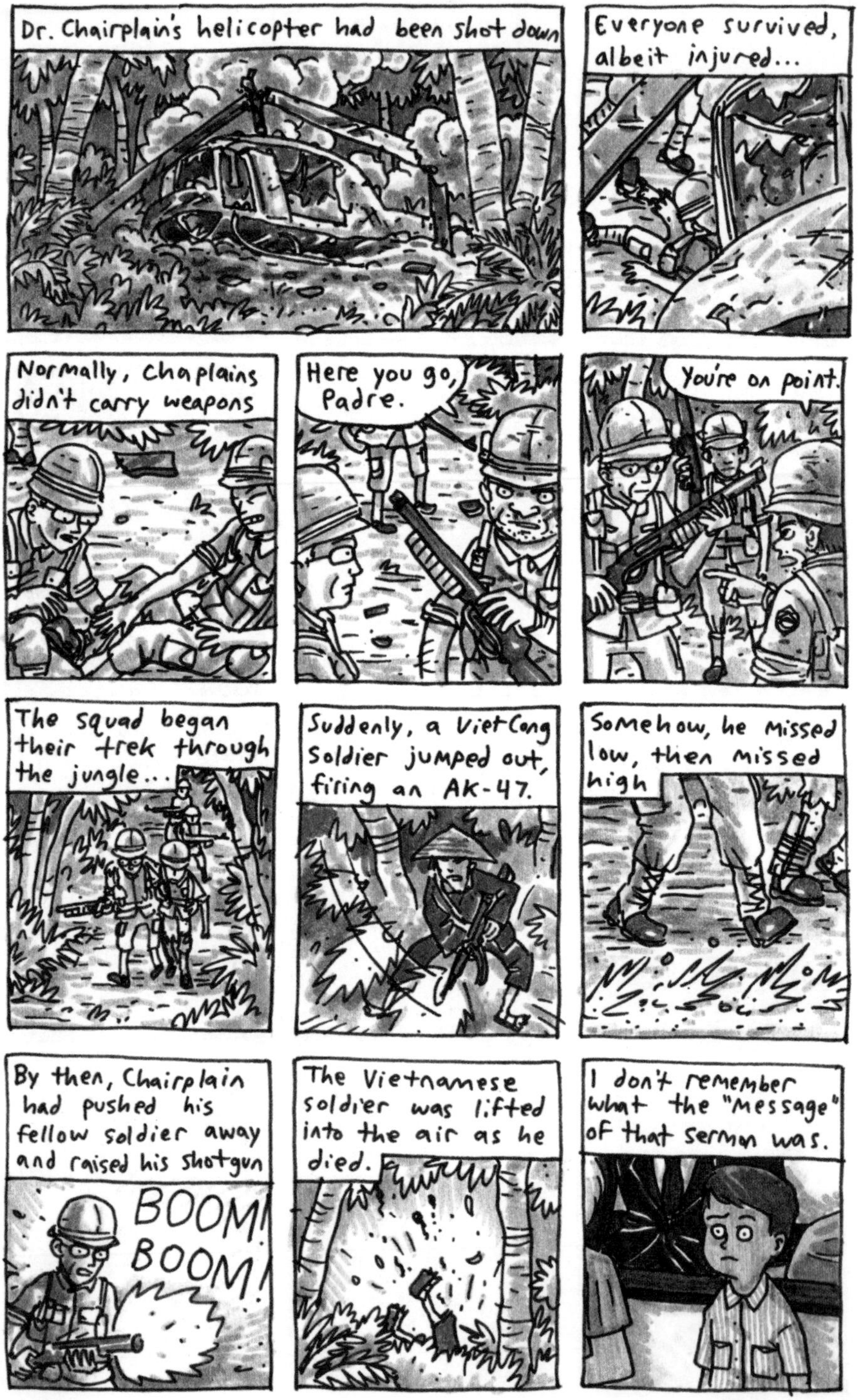
Dr. Chairplain's helicopter had been shot down
Everyone survived, albeit injured...
Normally, Chaplains didn't carry weapons
Here you go, Padre.
You're on point.
The squad began their trek through the jungle...
Suddenly, a Viet Cong soldier jumped out, firing an AK-47.
Somehow, he missed low, then missed high
By then, Chairplain had pushed his fellow soldier away and raised his shotgun
BOOM!
BOOM!
The Vietnamese soldier was lifted into the air as he died.
I don't remember what the "message" of that sermon was.

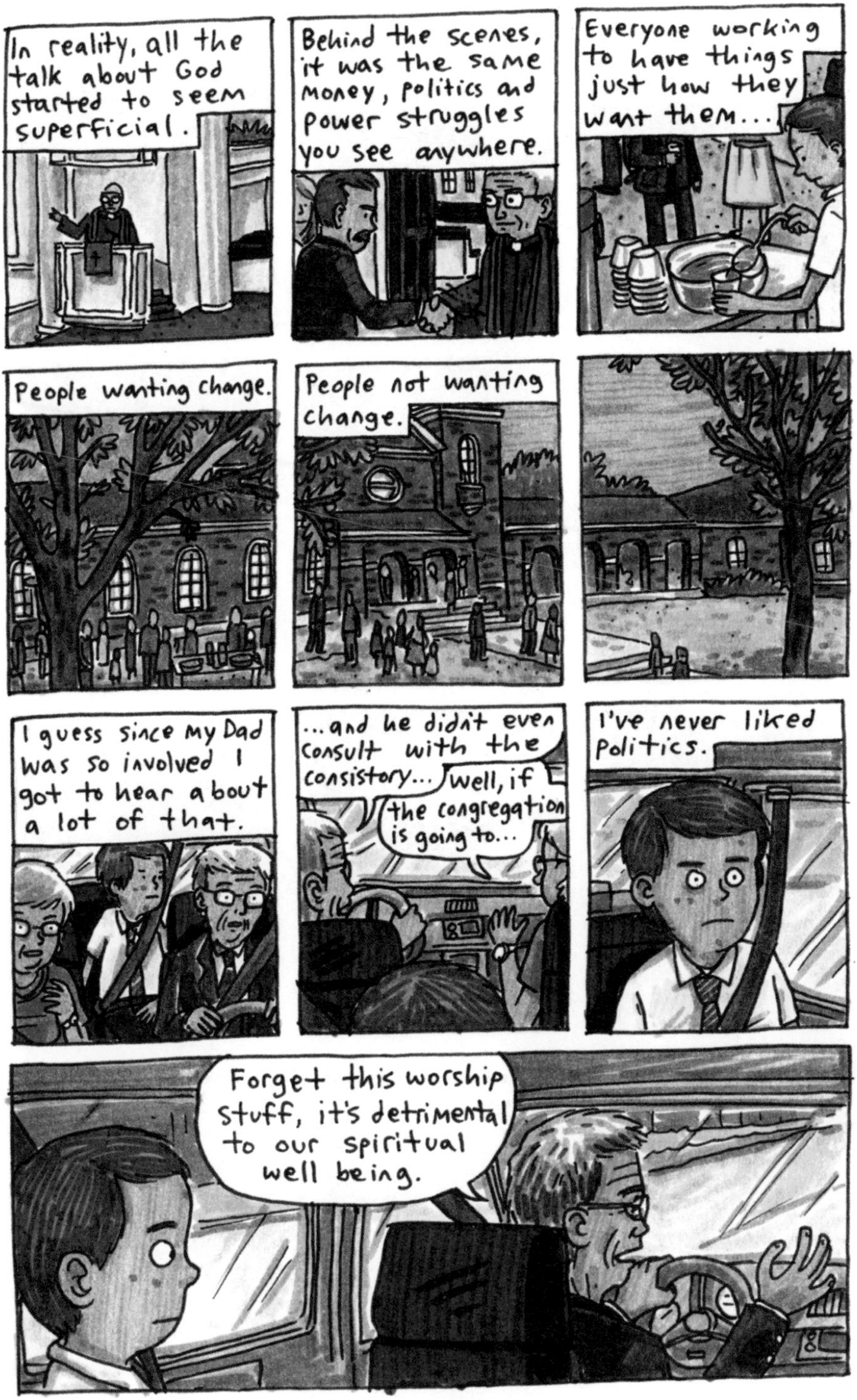
In reality, all the talk about God started to seem superficial.
Behind the scenes, it was the same money, politics and power struggles you see anywhere.
Everyone working to have things just how they want them...
People wanting change.
People not wanting change.
I guess since my Dad was so involved I got to hear about a lot of that.
...and he didn't even consult with the consistory...
Well, if the congregation is going to...
I've never liked Politics.
Forget this worship stuff, it's detrimental to our spiritual well being.

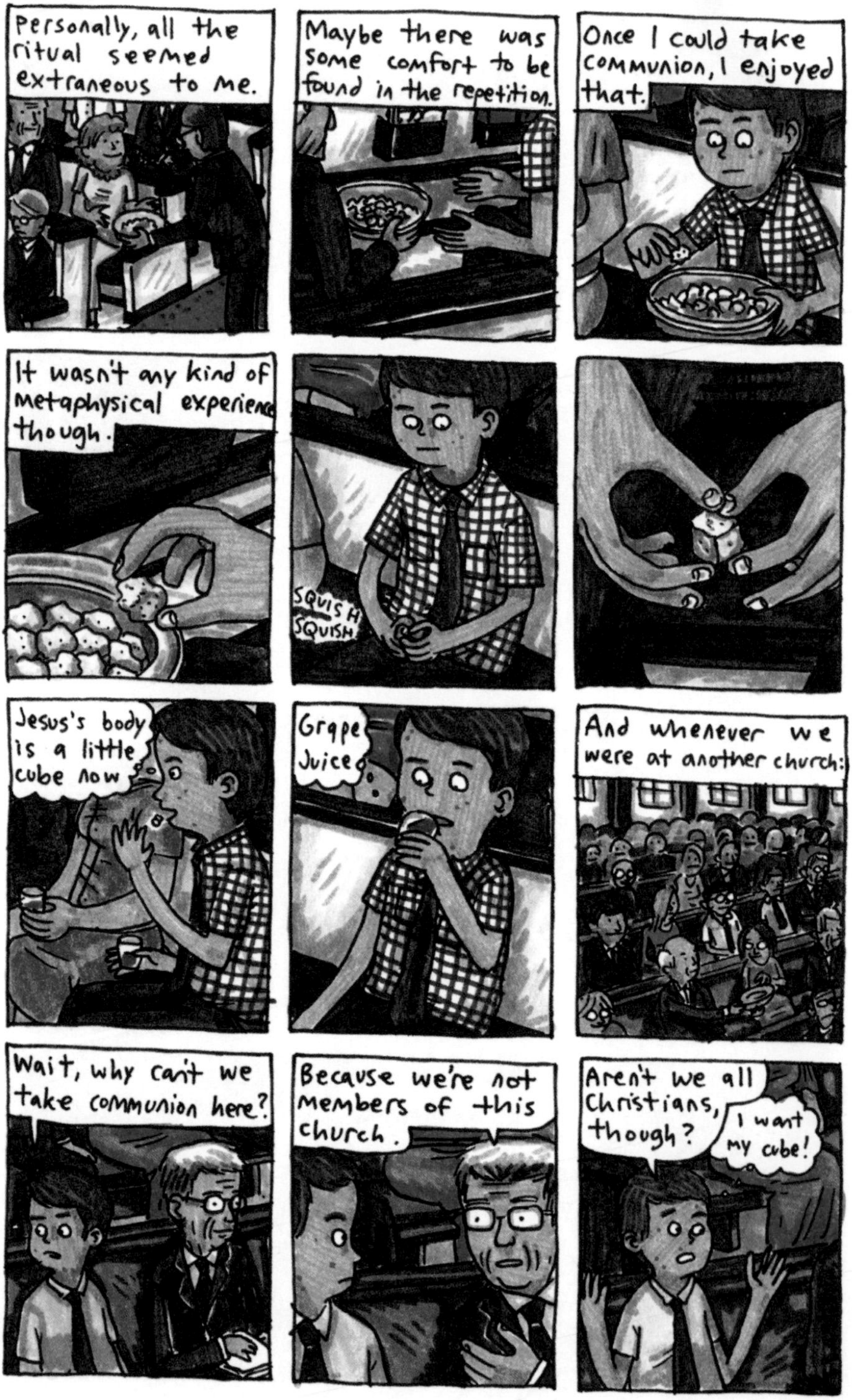
Personally, all the ritual seemed extraneous to me.
Maybe there was some comfort to be found in the repetition.
Once I could take communion, I enjoyed that.
It wasn't any kind of metaphysical experience though.
SQUISH
SQUISH
Jesus's body is a little cube now
Grape Juice
And whenever we were at another church:
Wait, why can't we take communion here?
Because we're not members of this church.
Aren't we all Christians, though?
I want my cube!

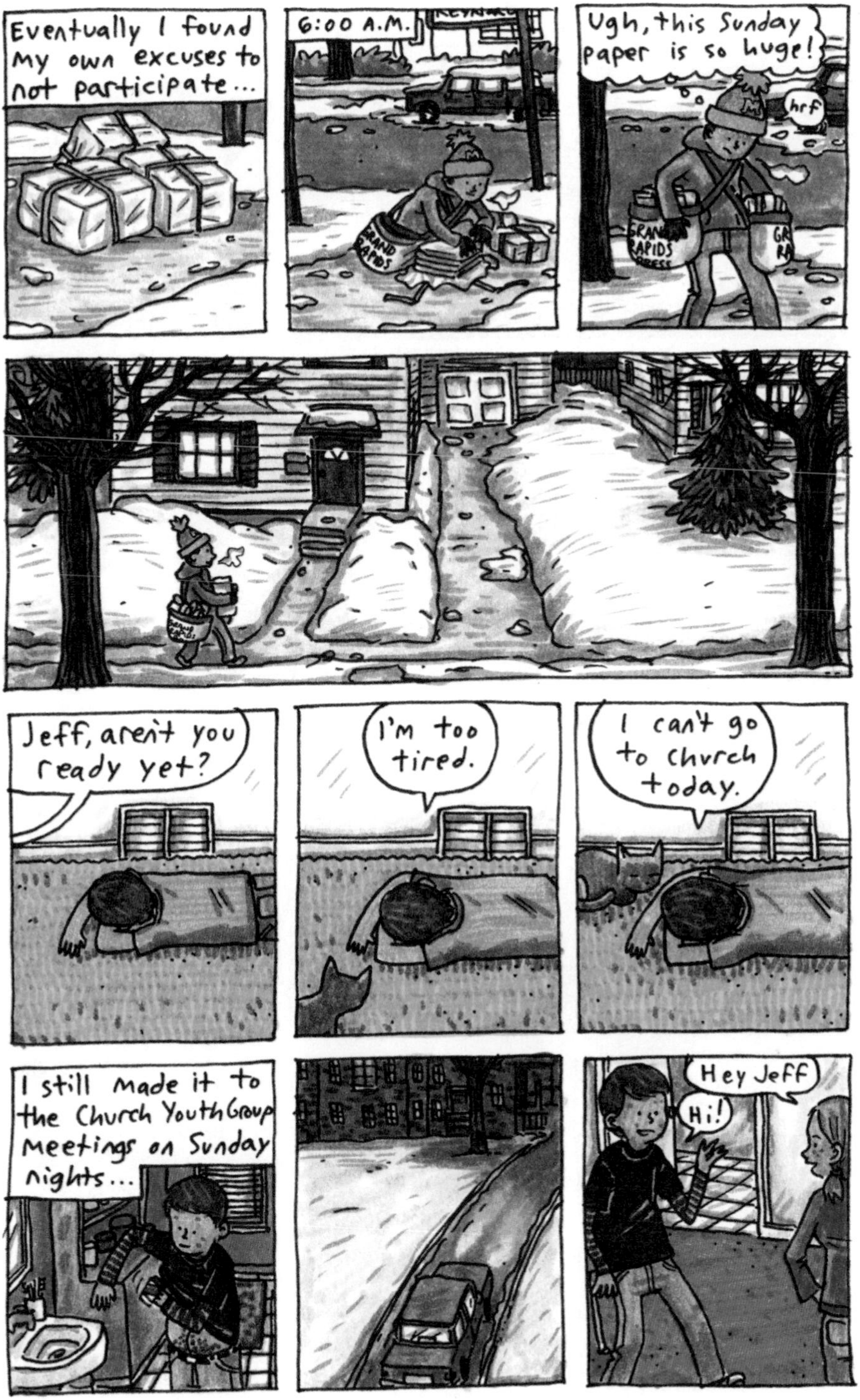
Eventually I found my own excuses to not participate...
6:00 A.M.
GRAND RAPIDS
Ugh, this Sunday paper is so huge!
hrf
GRAND RAPIDS
Jeff, aren't you ready yet?
I'm too tired.
I can't go to church today.
I still made it to the Church Youth Group meetings on Sunday nights...
Hey Jeff
Hi!

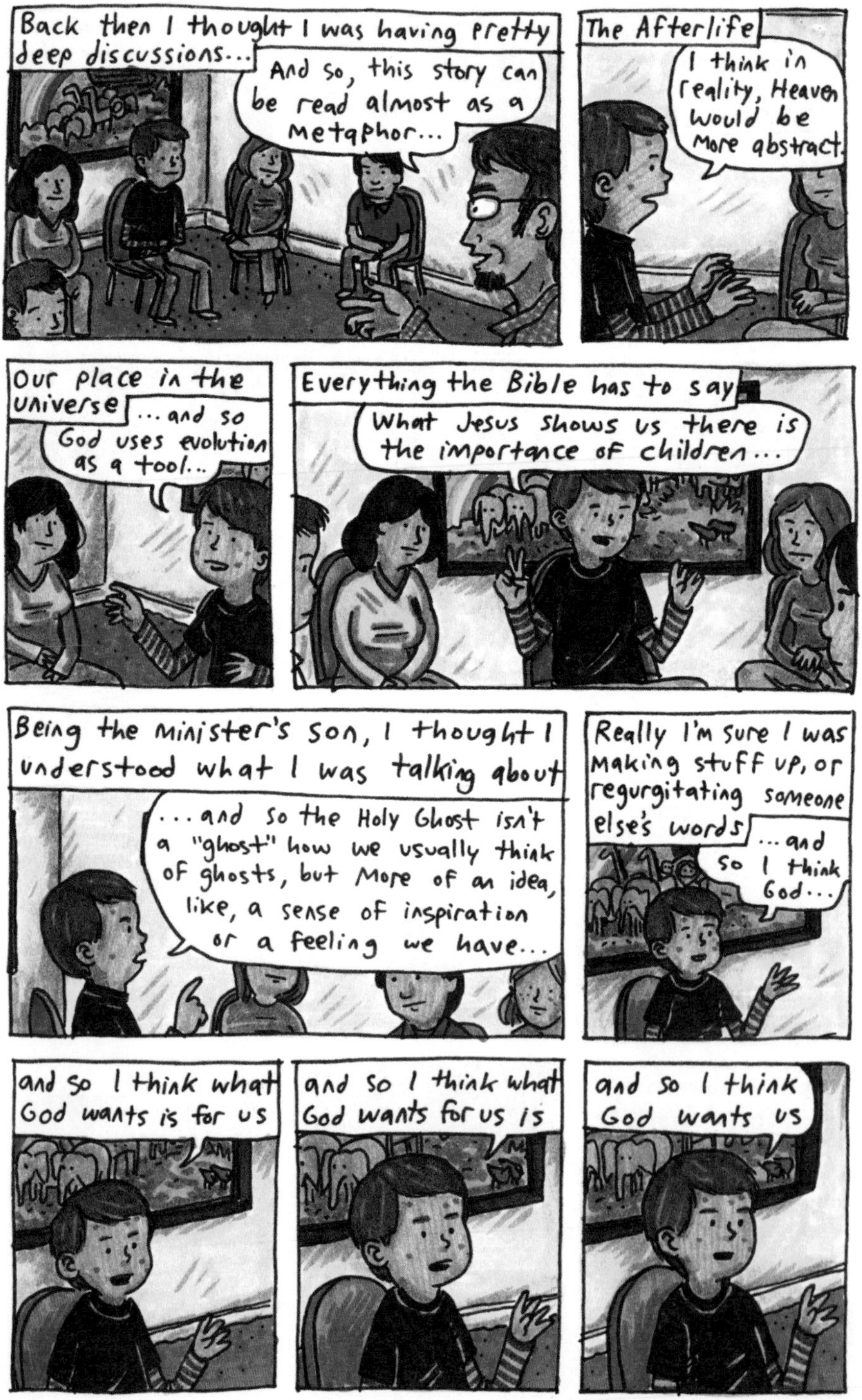
Back then I thought I was having pretty deep discussions...
And so, this story can be read almost as a metaphor...
The Afterlife
I think in reality, Heaven would be more abstract.
Our place in the universe
...and so God uses evolution as a tool...
Everything the Bible has to say
What Jesus shows us there is the importance of children...
Being the minister's son, I thought I understood what I was talking about
...and so the Holy Ghost isn't a "ghost" how we usually think of ghosts, but more of an idea, like, a sense of inspiration or a feeling we have...
Really I'm sure I was making stuff up, or regurgitating someone else's words
...and so I think God...
and so I think what God wants is for us
and so I think what God wants for us is
and so I think God wants us

Eventually repeated words started to lose their meaning

And I started to notice contradictions

Eye for an eye

Turn the other cheek

or Bible stories I just couldn't agree with

If you really have faith, you'll kill your son for me.

WTF, God?! Are you insane?

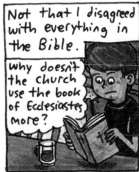

Not that I disagreed with everything in the Bible.

Why doesn't the church use the book of Ecclesiastes more?

It is fitting to eat and drink and find enjoyment in all the toil with which one toils under the sun the few days of life God gives us; for this is our lot.

All go to one place; all are from dust and all turn to dust again

This all makes a lot of sense...

Hm.

In his office, my Dad had a two hundred year old Dutch Bible.

I couldn't read it, of course.

It fascinated me as an object, an artifact

My high school had a class on comparative religion.

We'd already learned a lot of Greek mythology.

Now I learned about other creation myths, like the story of Gilgamesh.

And world religions, from Hinduism to Islam to Buddhism to Native American beliefs...

All these different religions shared so many elements...

CLUUB CLUUB

AIEEEEEE!

I could see them all coming from the same places...

UR.

We had to write a final paper about one religion.

SCIENTOLOGY

As a science fiction fan, I found the perfect subject

And anyone who reads the text goes CRAZY!

At first, it seemed like common sense, and I was intrigued

Literally, this means the study of science. It's fact-based religion!

SCIENTOLOGY

Soon, though...

Uh, what?

SCIENTOLOGY

Okaaaaaaaaay...

WHAT IS SCIENTOLOGY?

I never finished reading L. Ron Hubbard's "Mission Earth" sci-fi series, either.

RETURN

GRAN RAP PUBL LIBR

Sigh.

30

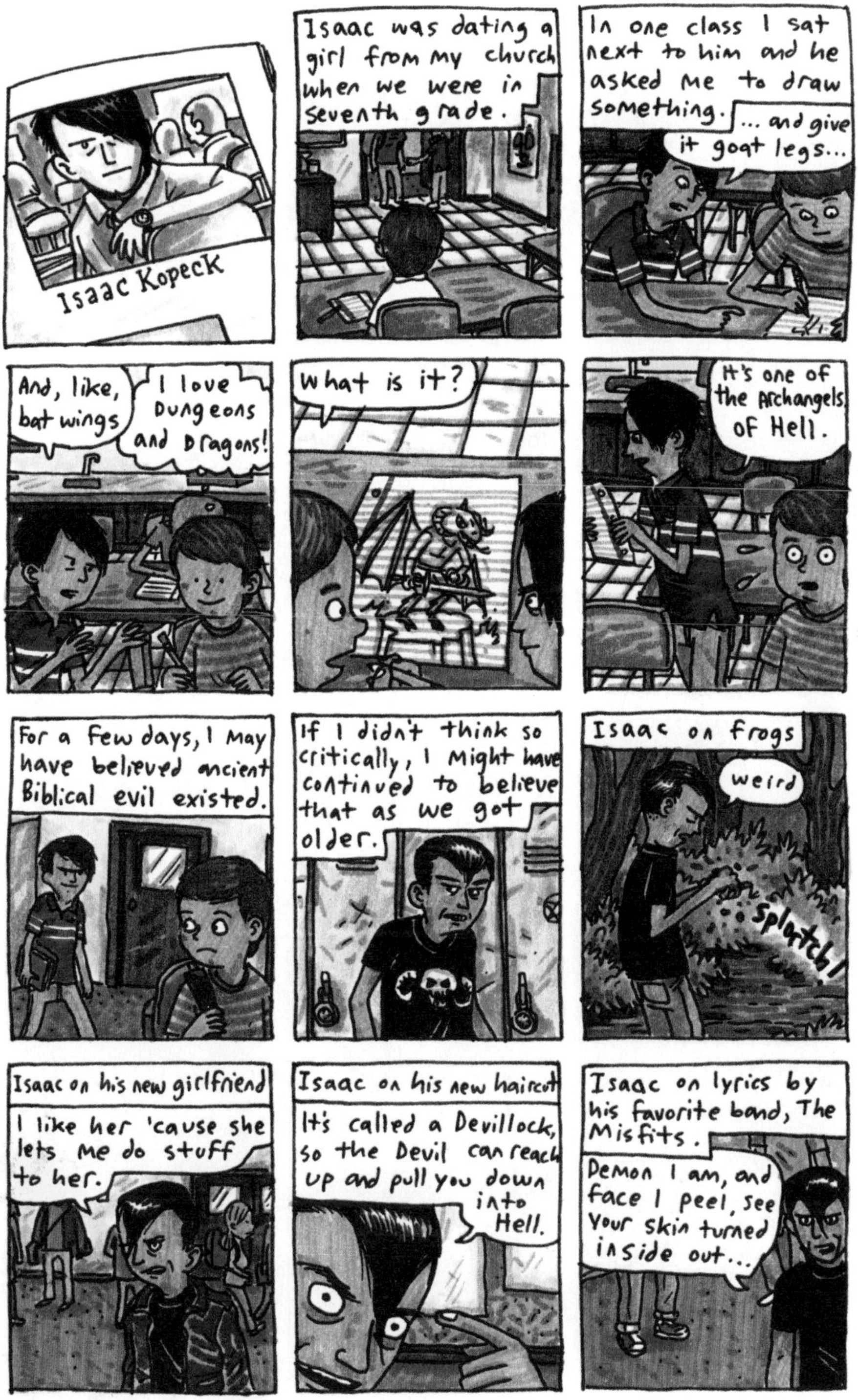
Isaac Kopeck
Isaac was dating a girl from my church when we were in seventh grade.
In one class I sat next to him and he asked me to draw something.
... and give it goat legs...
And, like, bat wings
I love Dungeons and Dragons!
What is it?
It's one of the Archangels of Hell.
For a few days, I may have believed ancient Biblical evil existed.
If I didn't think so critically, I might have continued to believe that as we got older.
Isaac on frogs
weird
Splatch!
Isaac on his new girlfriend
I like her 'cause she lets me do stuff to her.
Isaac on his new haircut
It's called a Devillock, so the Devil can reach up and pull you down into Hell.
Isaac on lyrics by his favorite band, The Misfits.
Demon I am, and face I peel, see your skin turned inside out...

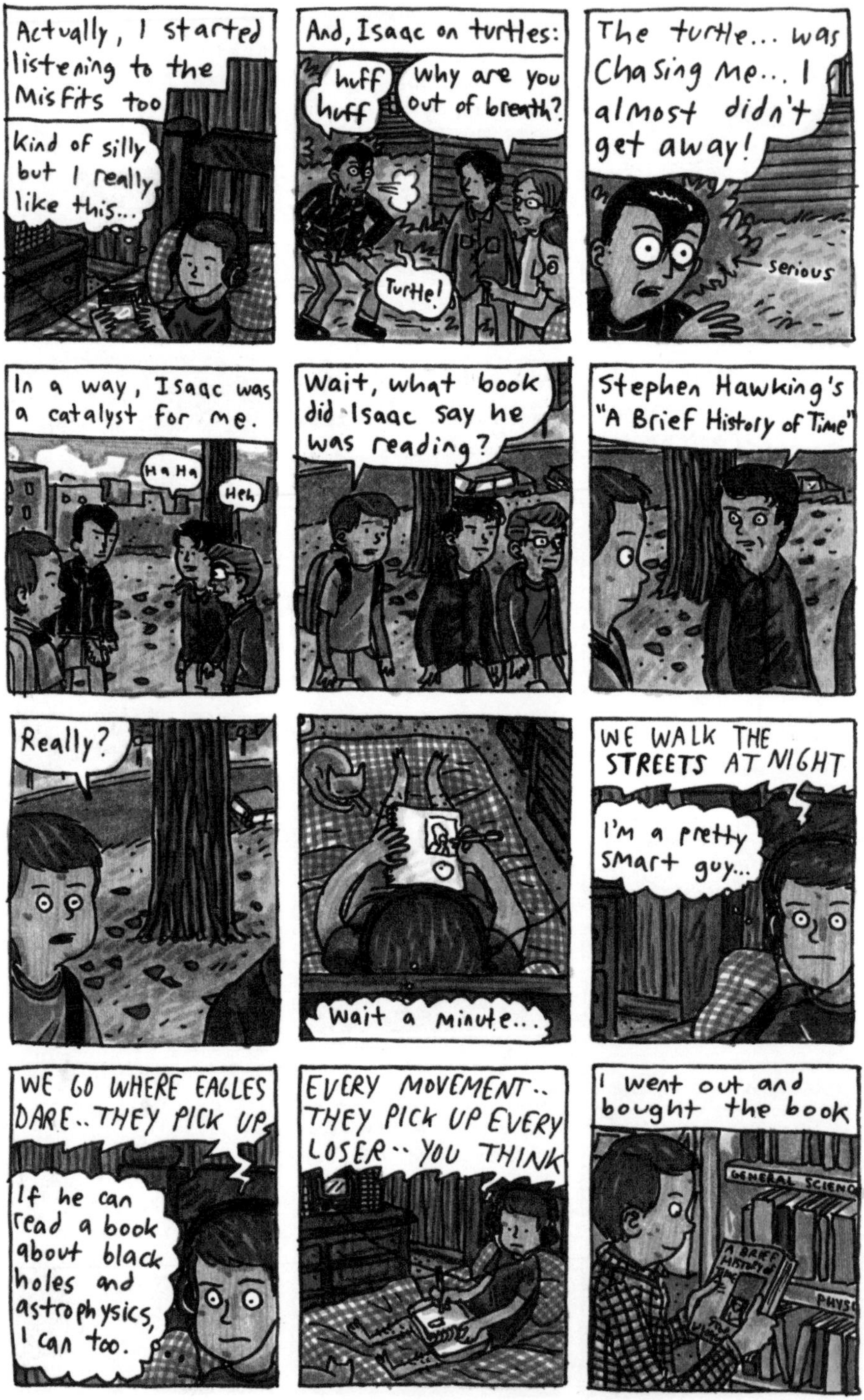
Actually, I started listening to the Misfits too
Kind of silly but I really like this...
And, Isaac on turtles:
huff huff
Why are you out of breath?
Turtle!
The turtle... was chasing me... I almost didn't get away!
serious
In a way, Isaac was a catalyst for me.
Ha Ha
Heh
Wait, what book did Isaac say he was reading?
Stephen Hawking's "A Brief History of Time"
Really?
Wait a minute...
WE WALK THE STREETS AT NIGHT
I'm a pretty smart guy...
WE GO WHERE EAGLES DARE.. THEY PICK UP
If he can read a book about black holes and astrophysics, I can too.
EVERY MOVEMENT.. THEY PICK UP EVERY LOSER.. YOU THINK
I went out and bought the book
GENERAL SCIENC
A BRIEF HISTORY of TIME
PHYSI

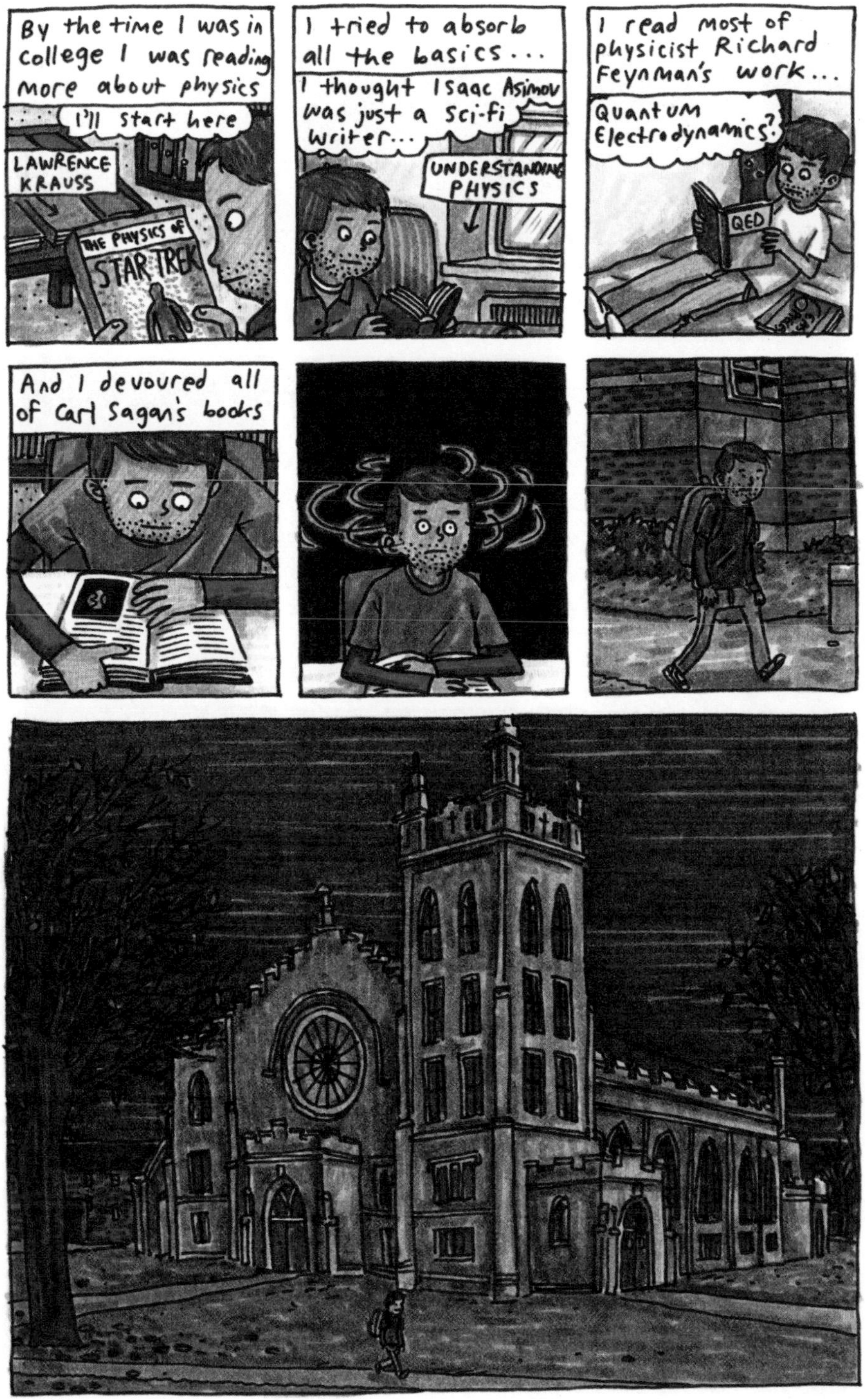
By the time I was in college I was reading more about physics
I'll start here
LAWRENCE KRAUSS
THE PHYSICS OF STAR TREK
I tried to absorb all the basics...
I thought Isaac Asimov was just a sci-fi writer...
UNDERSTANDING PHYSICS
I read most of physicist Richard Feynman's work...
Quantum Electrodynamics?
QED
And I devoured all of Carl Sagan's books

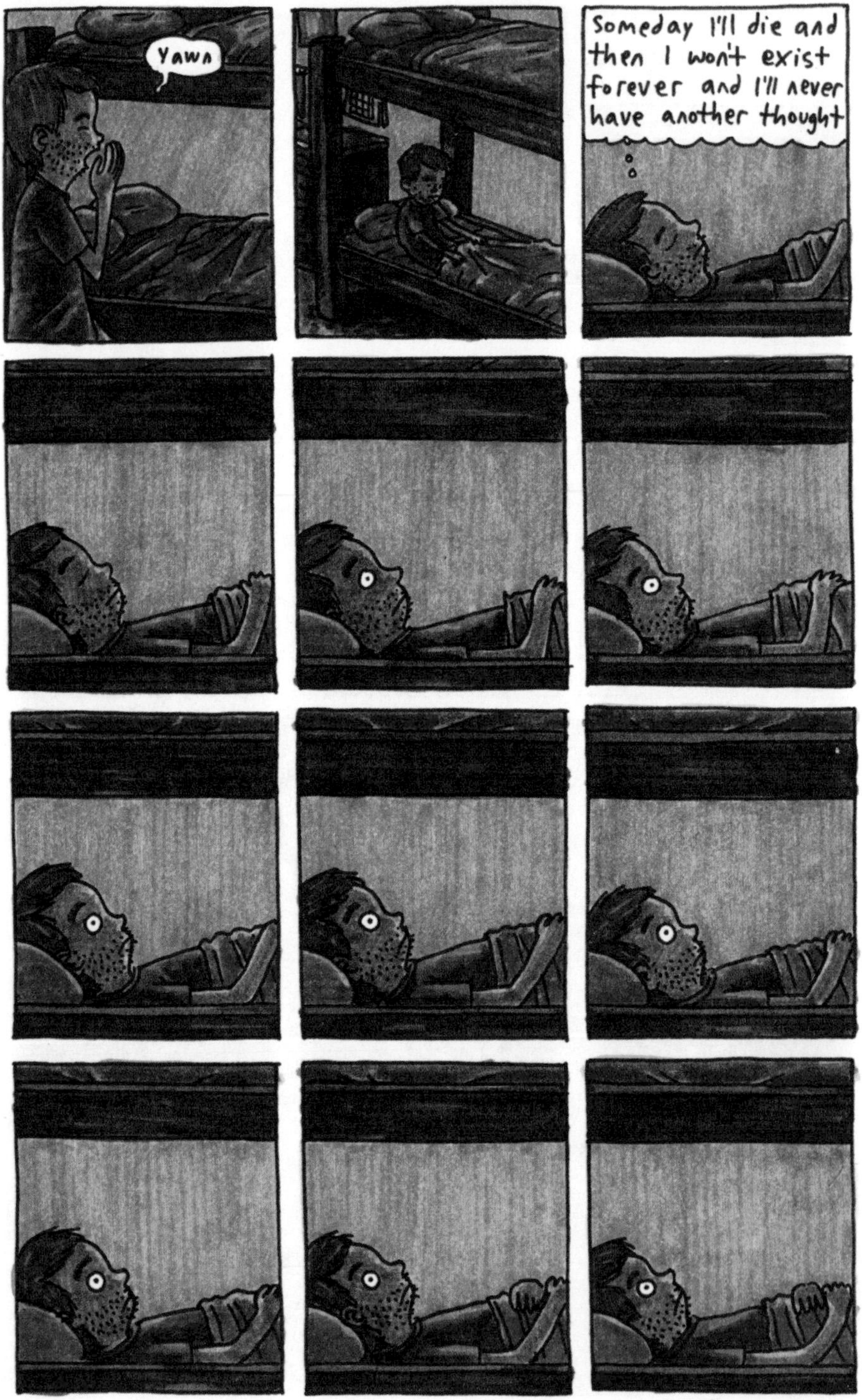
Yawn
Someday I'll die and then I won't exist forever and I'll never have another thought

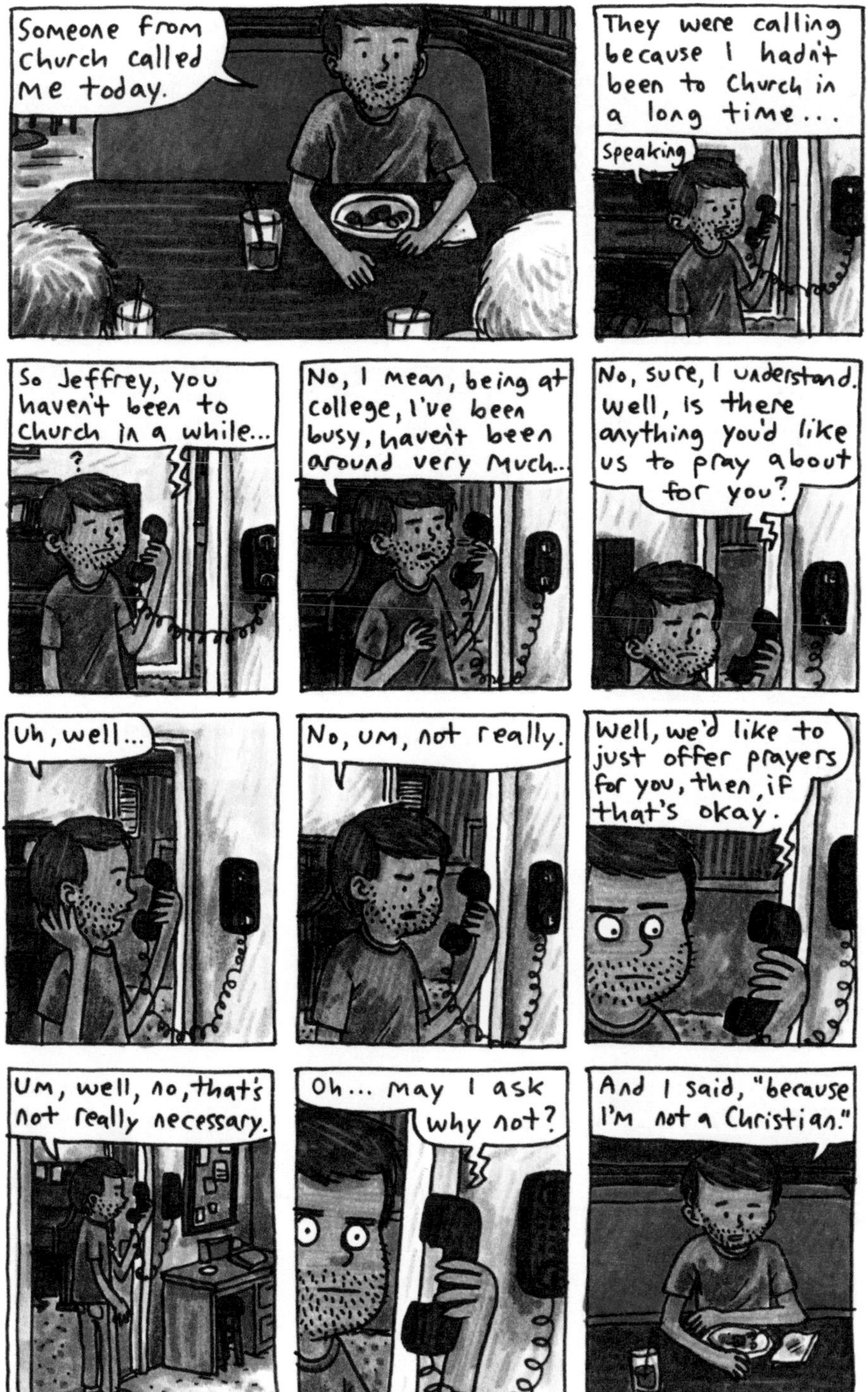

Someone from church called me today.
They were calling because I hadn't been to church in a long time...
Speaking
So Jeffrey, you haven't been to church in a while...
?
No, I mean, being at college, I've been busy, haven't been around very much...
No, sure, I understand. Well, is there anything you'd like us to pray about for you?
Uh, well...
No, um, not really.
Well, we'd like to just offer prayers for you, then, if that's okay.
Um, well, no, that's not really necessary.
Oh... May I ask why not?
And I said, "because I'm not a Christian."

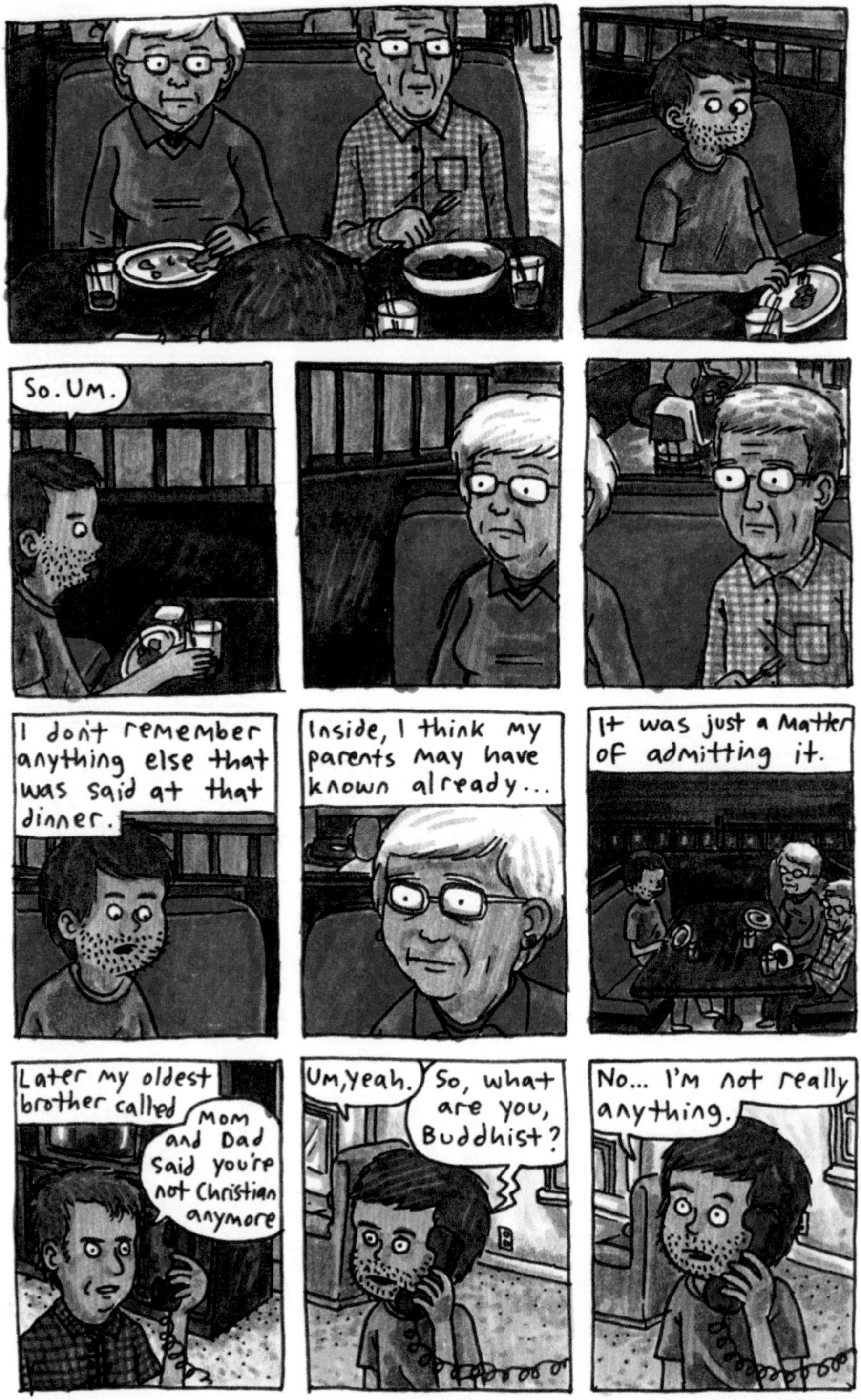
So. Um.
I don't remember anything else that was said at that dinner.
Inside, I think my parents may have known already...
It was just a Matter of admitting it.
Later my oldest brother called
Mom and Dad said you're not Christian anymore
Um, yeah.
So, what are you, Buddhist?
No... I'm not really anything.

CAN YOU FEEL JESUS IN YOUR HEART?
RARRRRRRRR!
JEFF?
JEFF, YOU ARE A BAD PERSON. YOU ARE A HORRIBLE PERSON.
RARRRRRRR!
RARRRRRRR!

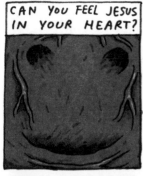

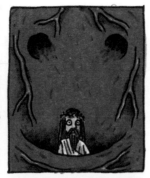

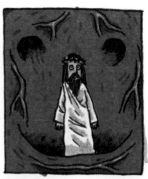

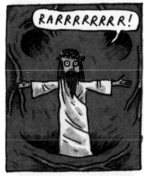

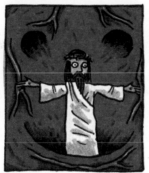

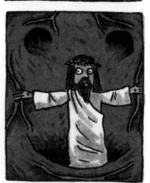

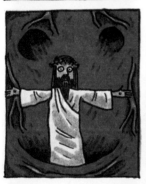

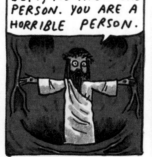

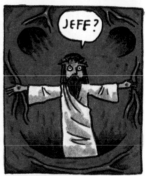

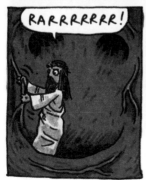

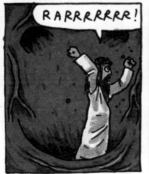

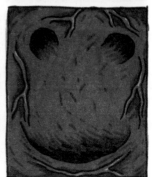

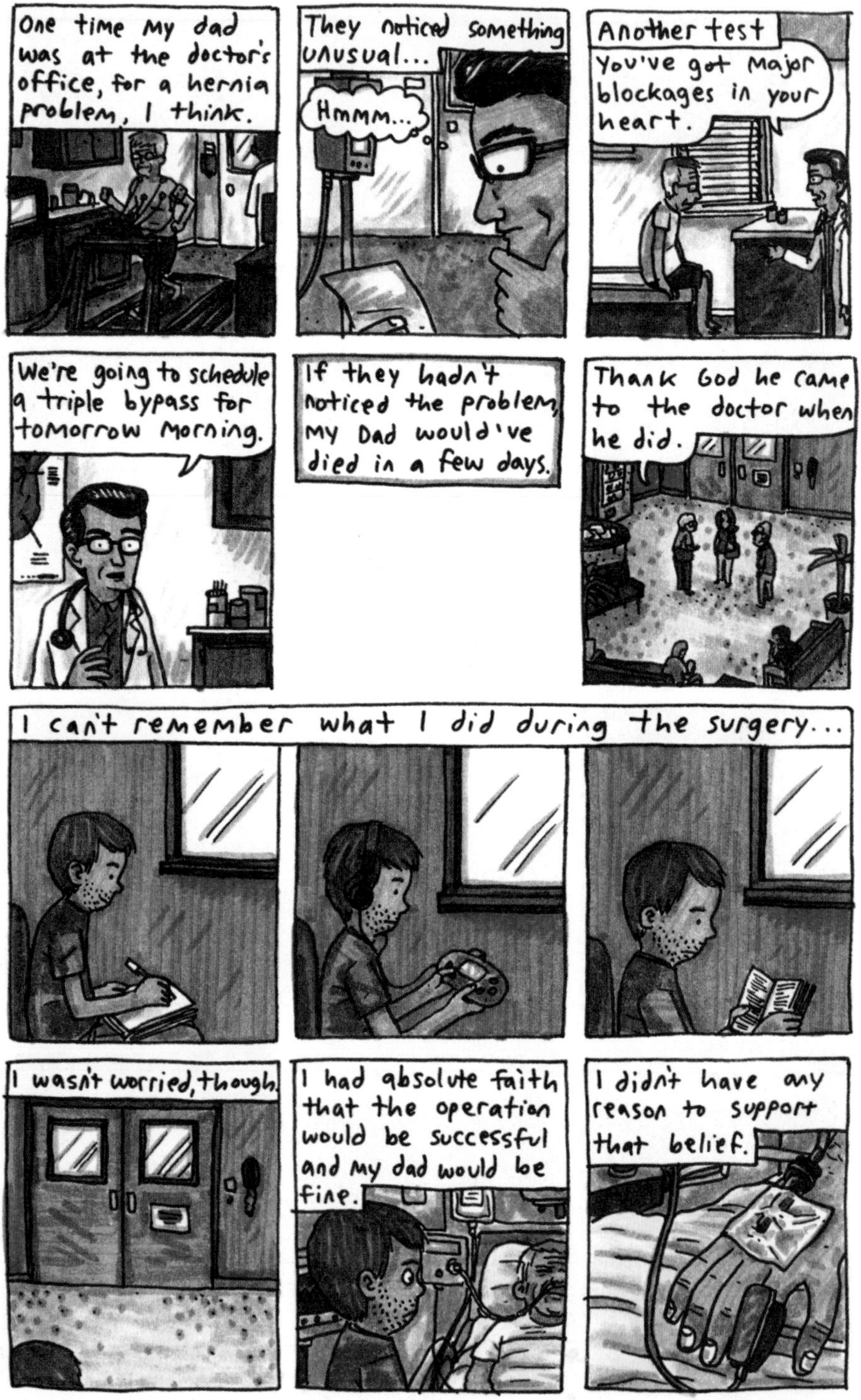
One time my dad was at the doctor's office, for a hernia problem, I think.
They noticed something unusual...
Hmmm...
Another test
You've got major blockages in your heart.
We're going to schedule a triple bypass for tomorrow morning.
If they hadn't noticed the problem, my Dad would've died in a few days.
Thank God he came to the doctor when he did.
I can't remember what I did during the surgery...
I wasn't worried, though.
I had absolute faith that the operation would be successful and my dad would be fine.
I didn't have any reason to support that belief.

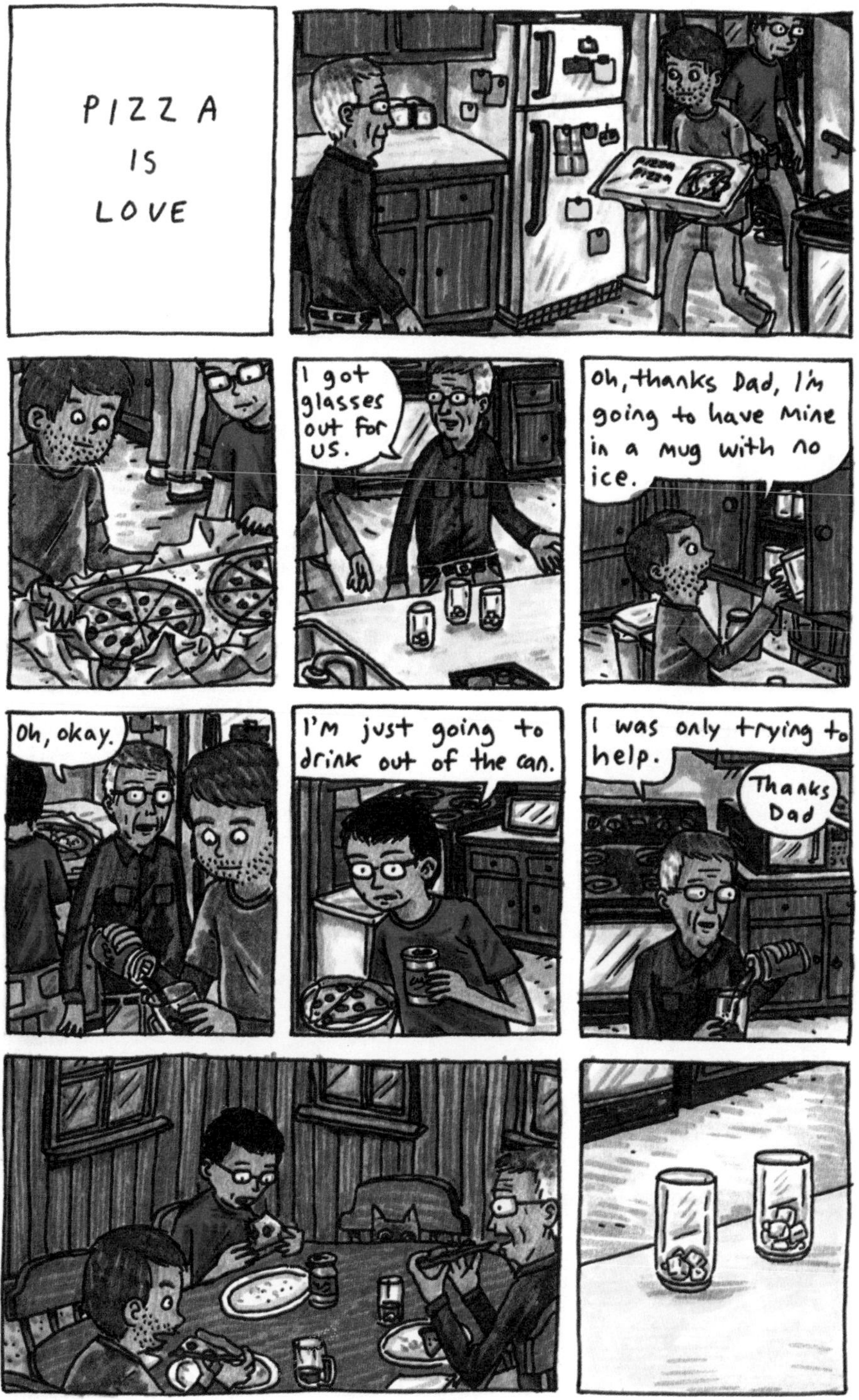
PIZZA IS LOVE
I got glasses out for us.
Oh, thanks Dad, I'm going to have mine in a mug with no ice.
Oh, okay.
I'm just going to drink out of the can.
I was only trying to help.
Thanks Dad

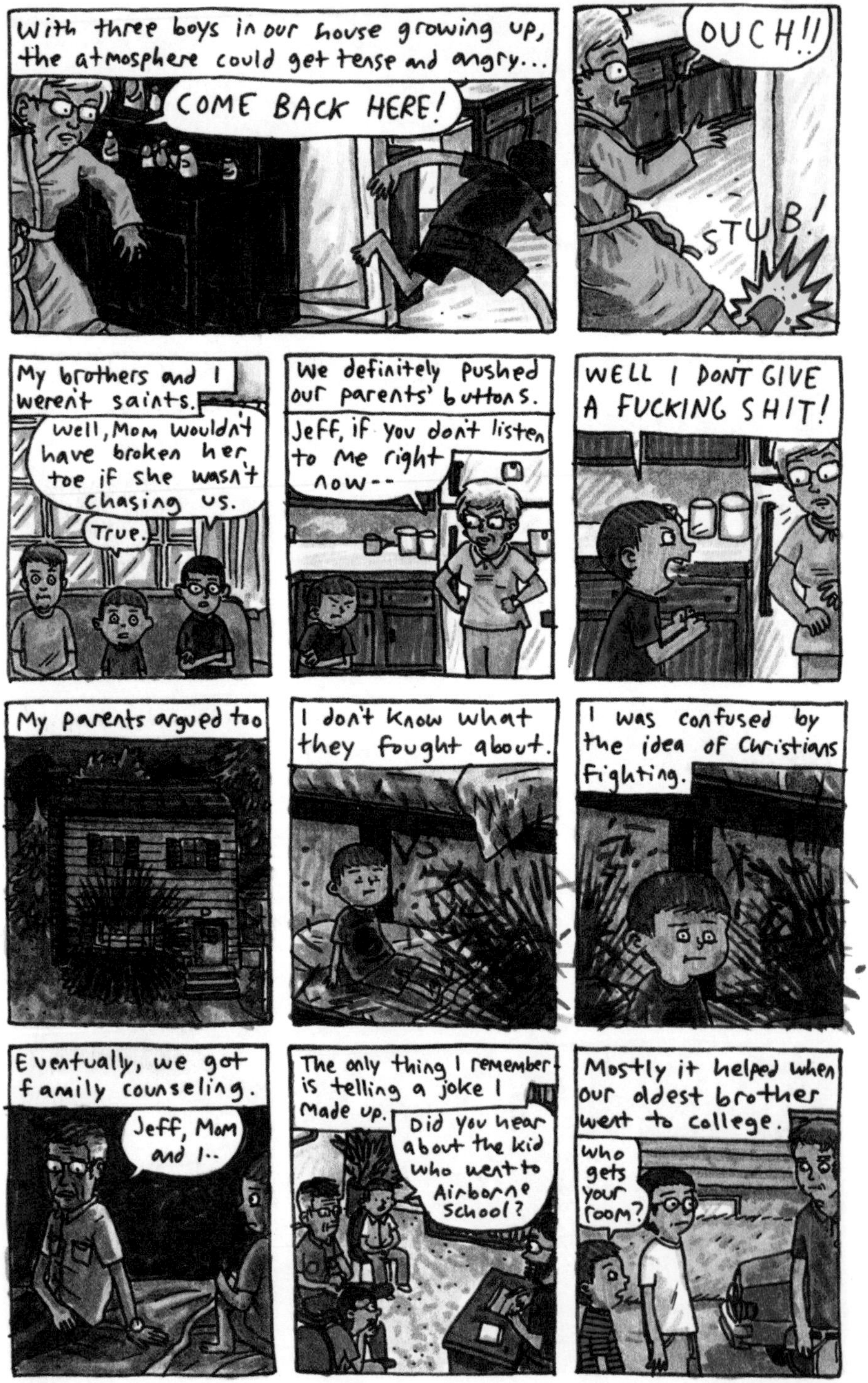
With three boys in our house growing up, the atmosphere could get tense and angry...
COME BACK HERE!
OUCH!!
STUB!
My brothers and I weren't saints.
Well, Mom wouldn't have broken her toe if she wasn't chasing us.
True.
We definitely pushed our parents' buttons.
Jeff, if you don't listen to me right now--
WELL I DON'T GIVE A FUCKING SHIT!
My parents argued too
I don't know what they fought about.
I was confused by the idea of Christians fighting.
Eventually, we got family counseling.
Jeff, Mom and I..
The only thing I remember is telling a joke I made up.
Did you hear about the kid who went to Airborne School?
Mostly it helped when our oldest brother went to college.
Who gets your room?

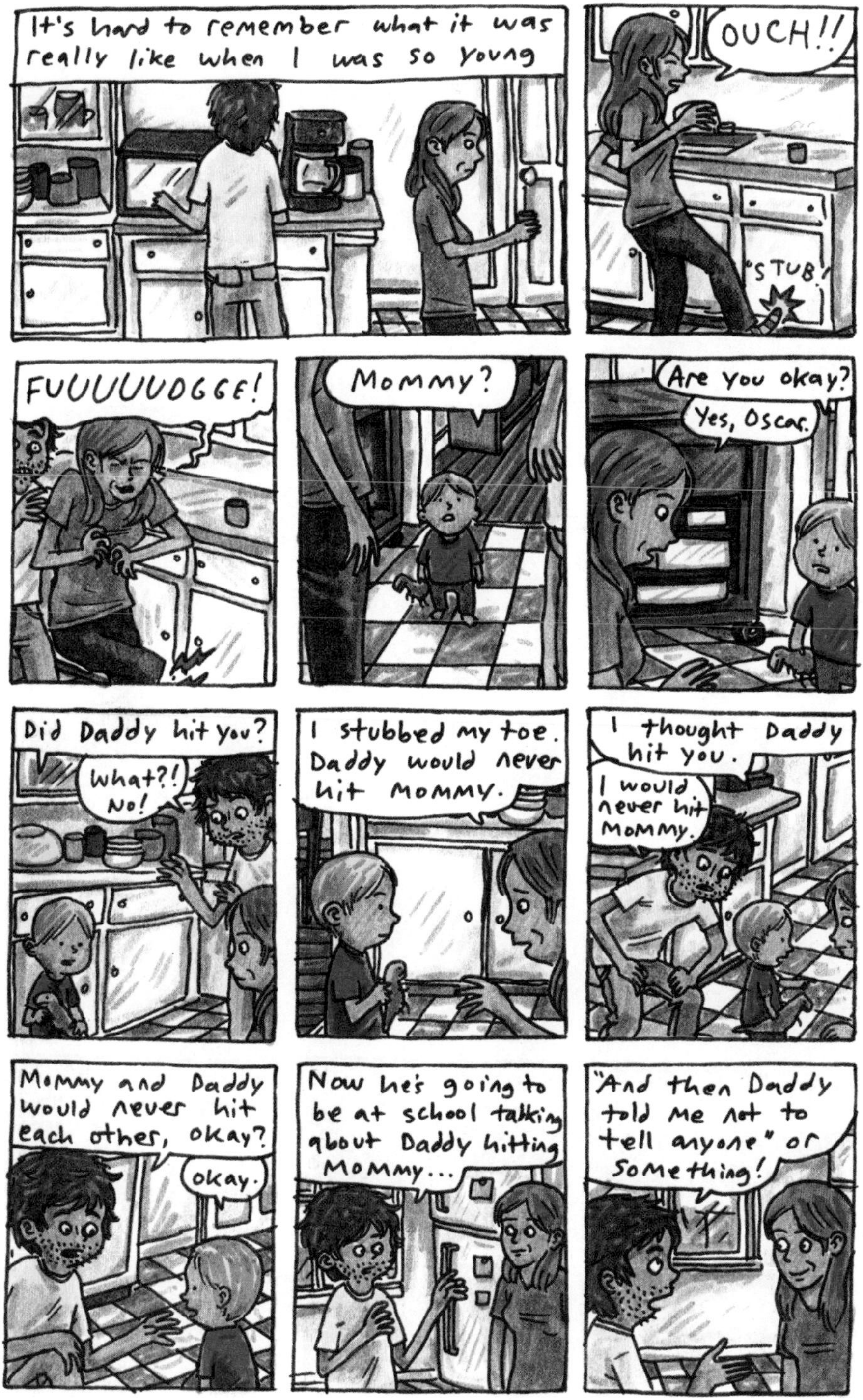
It's hard to remember what it was really like when I was so young
OUCH!!
STUB!
FUUUUUUDGGE!
Mommy?
Are you okay?
Yes, Oscar.
Did Daddy hit you?
What?! No!
I stubbed my toe. Daddy would never hit Mommy.
I thought Daddy hit you.
I would never hit Mommy.
Mommy and Daddy would never hit each other, okay?
okay.
Now he's going to be at school talking about Daddy hitting Mommy...
"And then Daddy told me not to tell anyone" or something!

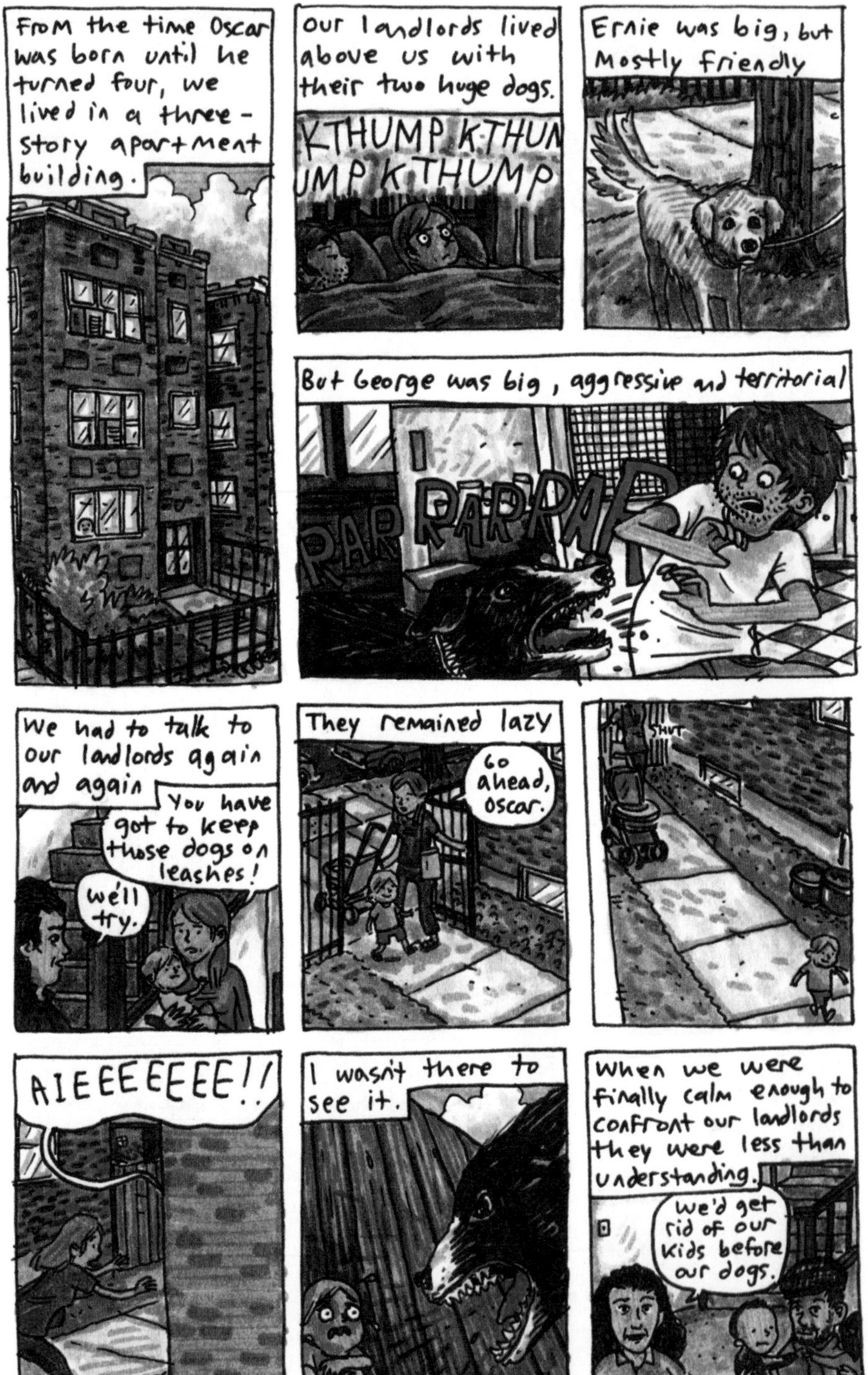
From the time Oscar was born until he turned four, we lived in a three-story apartment building.
Our landlords lived above us with their two huge dogs.
KTHUMP KTHUMP KTHUMP KTHUMP
Ernie was big, but mostly friendly
But George was big, aggressive and territorial
RAR RAR RAR RAR
We had to talk to our landlords again and again
You have got to keep those dogs on leashes!
We'll try.
They remained lazy
Go ahead, Oscar.
SHUT
AIEEEEEEE!!
I wasn't there to see it.
When we were finally calm enough to confront our landlords they were less than understanding.
We'd get rid of our kids before our dogs.

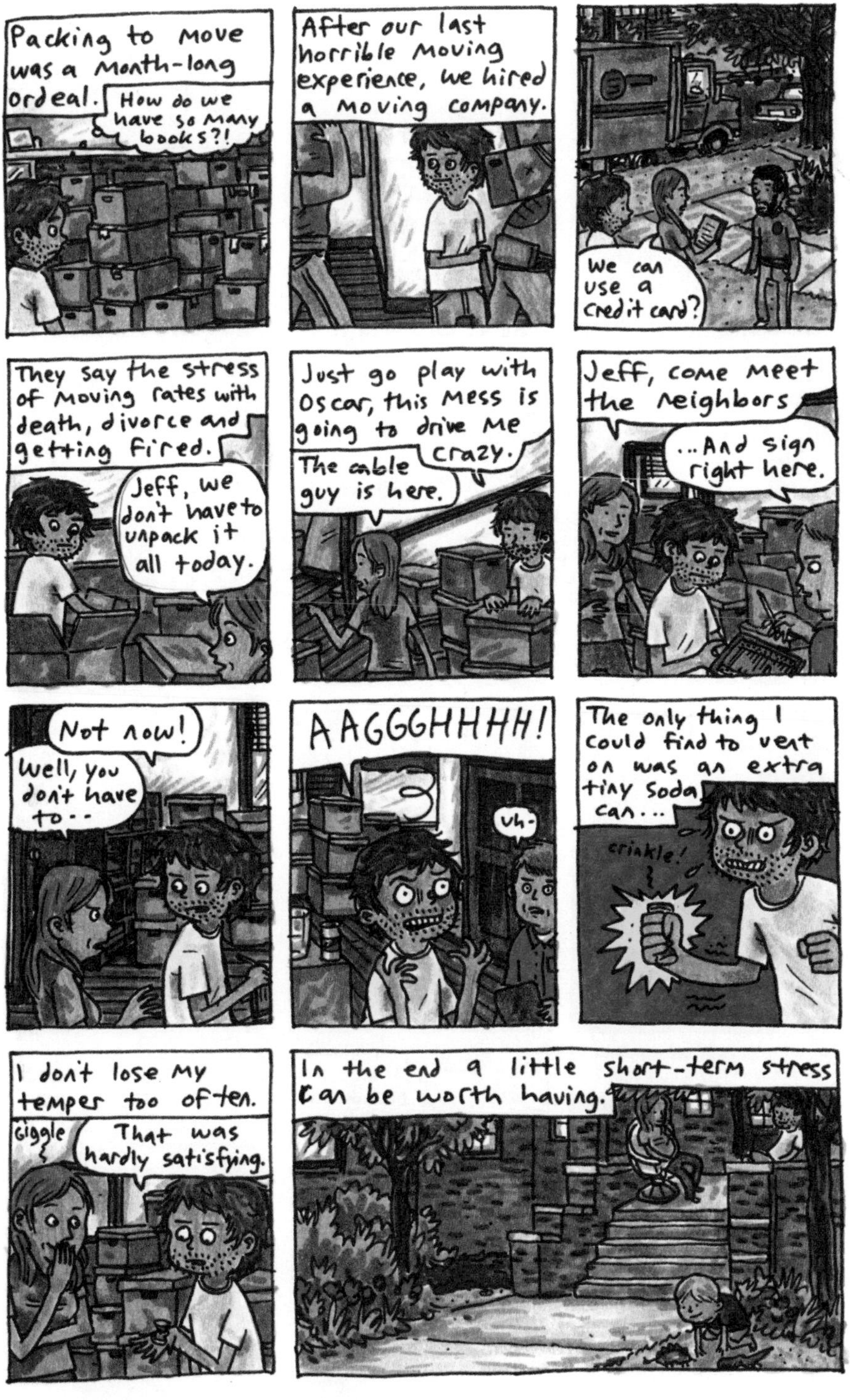

Packing to move was a month-long ordeal.
How do we have so many books?!
After our last horrible moving experience, we hired a moving company.
We can use a credit card?
They say the stress of moving rates with death, divorce and getting fired.
Jeff, we don't have to unpack it all today.
Just go play with Oscar, this mess is going to drive me crazy.
The cable guy is here.
Jeff, come meet the neighbors
...And sign right here.
Not now!
Well, you don't have to--
AAGGGHHHH!
Uh-
The only thing I could find to vent on was an extra tiny soda can...
crinkle!
I don't lose my temper too often.
Giggle
That was hardly satisfying.
In the end a little short-term stress can be worth having.

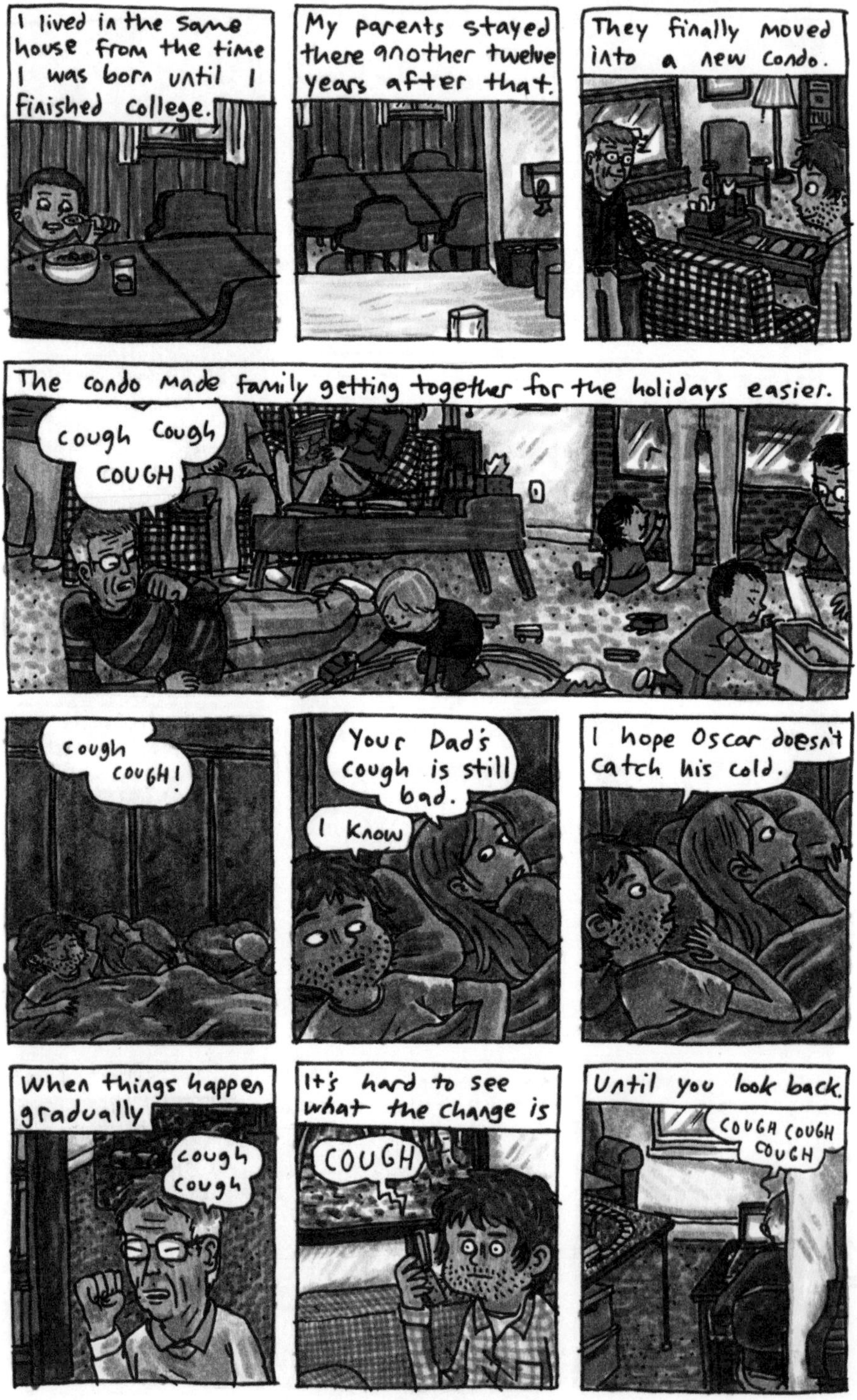
I lived in the same house from the time I was born until I finished college.
My parents stayed there another twelve years after that.
They finally moved into a new condo.
The condo made family getting together for the holidays easier.
cough cough COUGH
cough COUGH!
Your Dad's cough is still bad.
I know
I hope Oscar doesn't catch his cold.
When things happen gradually
cough cough
It's hard to see what the change is
COUGH
Until you look back.
COUGH COUGH COUGH

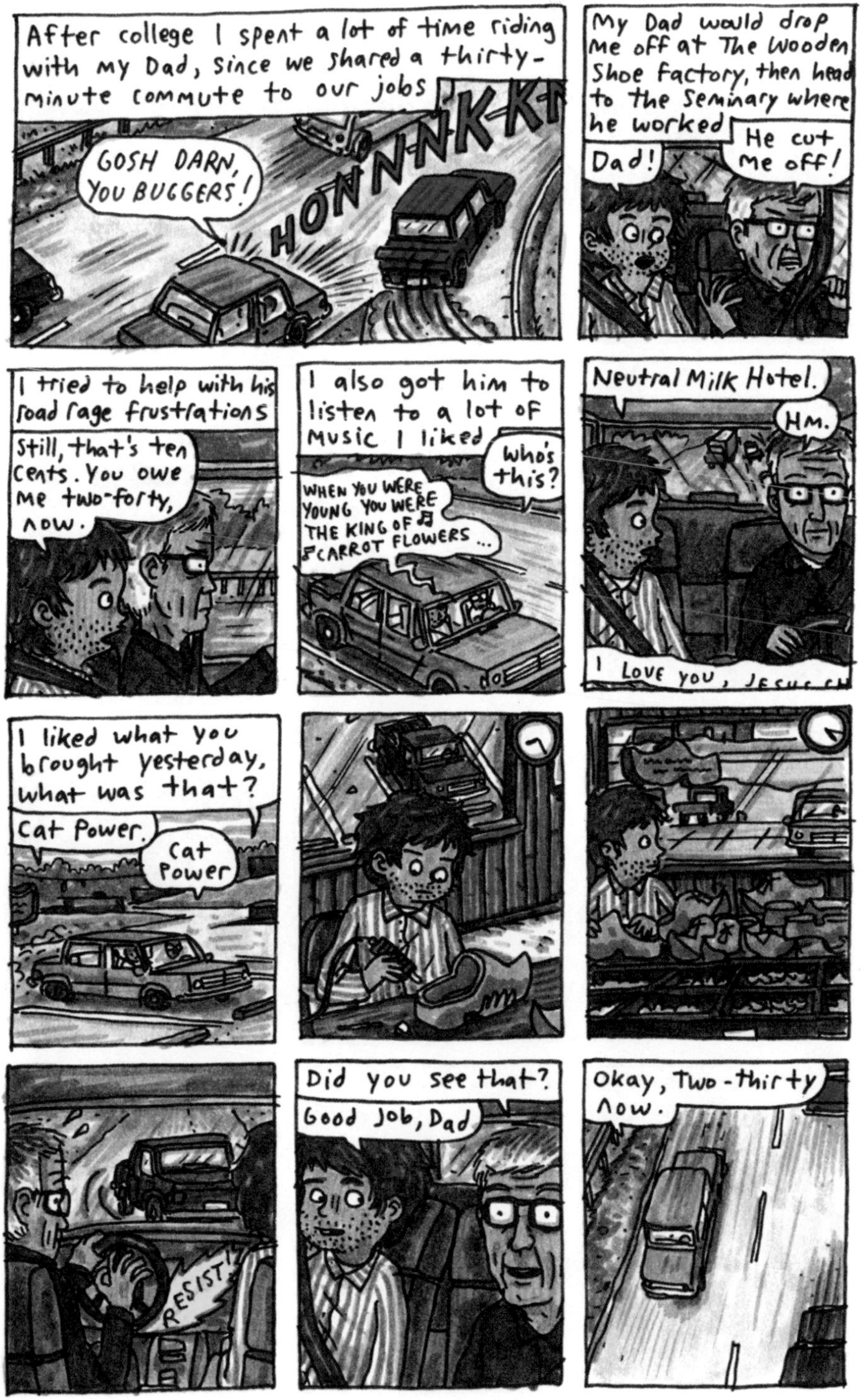

After college I spent a lot of time riding with my Dad, since we shared a thirty-minute commute to our jobs
HONNNNKKKK
GOSH DARN, YOU BUGGERS!
My Dad would drop me off at The Wooden Shoe Factory, then head to the Seminary where he worked
Dad!
He cut me off!
I tried to help with his road rage frustrations
Still, that's ten cents. You owe me two-forty, now.
I also got him to listen to a lot of music I liked
Who's this?
WHEN YOU WERE YOUNG YOU WERE THE KING OF CARROT FLOWERS...
Neutral Milk Hotel.
Hm.
I LOVE YOU,
I liked what you brought yesterday, what was that?
Cat Power.
Cat Power
RESIST!
Did you see that?
Good Job, Dad
Okay, Two-thirty now.

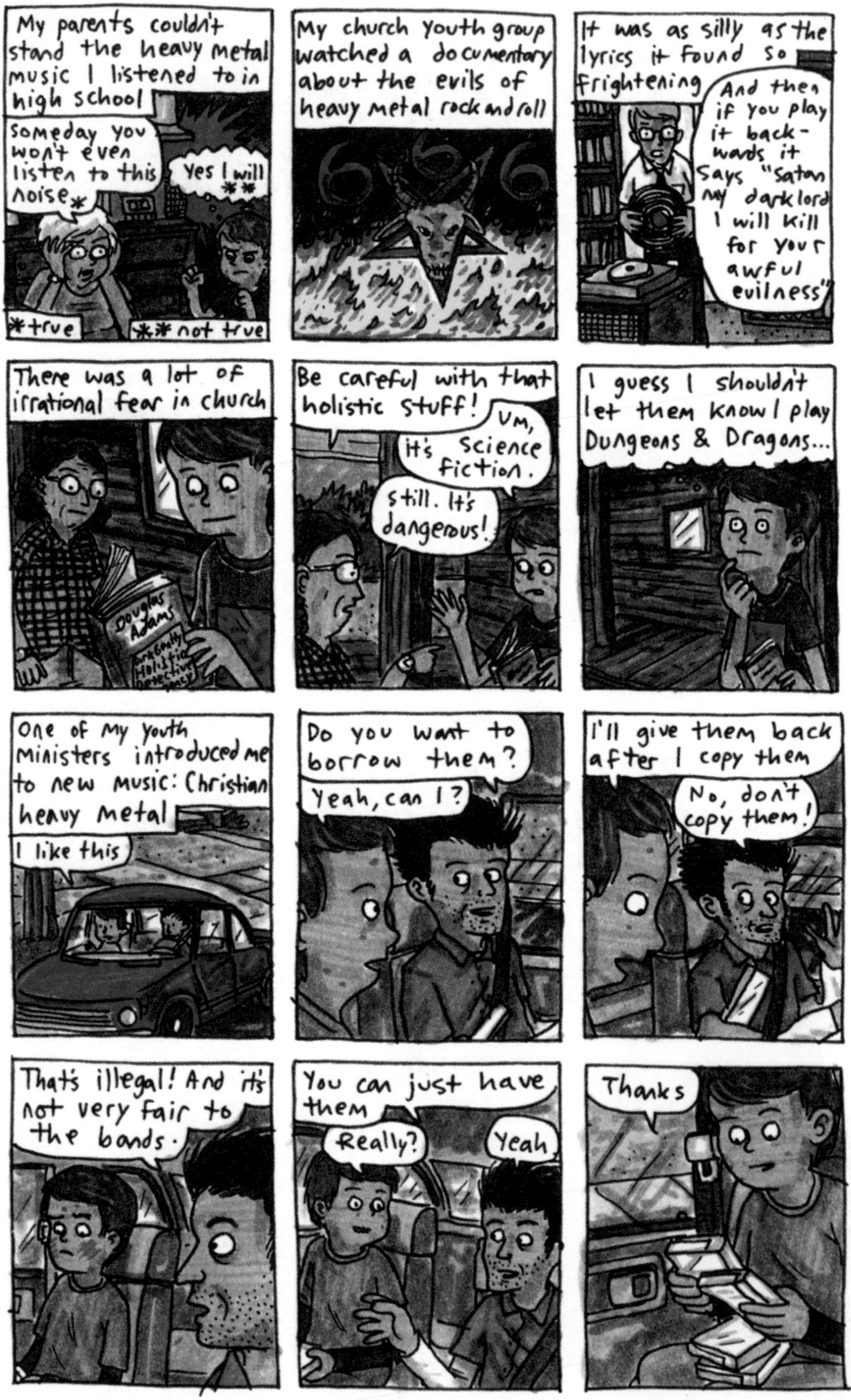
My parents couldn't stand the heavy metal music I listened to in high school
Someday you won't even listen to this noise*
Yes I will **
*true
**not true
My church youth group watched a documentary about the evils of heavy metal rock and roll
It was as silly as the lyrics it found so frightening
And then if you play it back-wards it says "Satan my dark lord I will kill for your awful evilness"
There was a lot of irrational fear in church
Douglas Adams
Dirk Gently's Holistic Detective Agency
Be careful with that holistic stuff!
Um, it's science fiction.
Still. It's dangerous!
I guess I shouldn't let them know I play Dungeons & Dragons...
One of my youth ministers introduced me to new music: Christian heavy metal
I like this
Do you want to borrow them?
Yeah, can I?
I'll give them back after I copy them
No, don't copy them!
That's illegal! And it's not very fair to the bands.
You can just have them
Really?
Yeah
Thanks

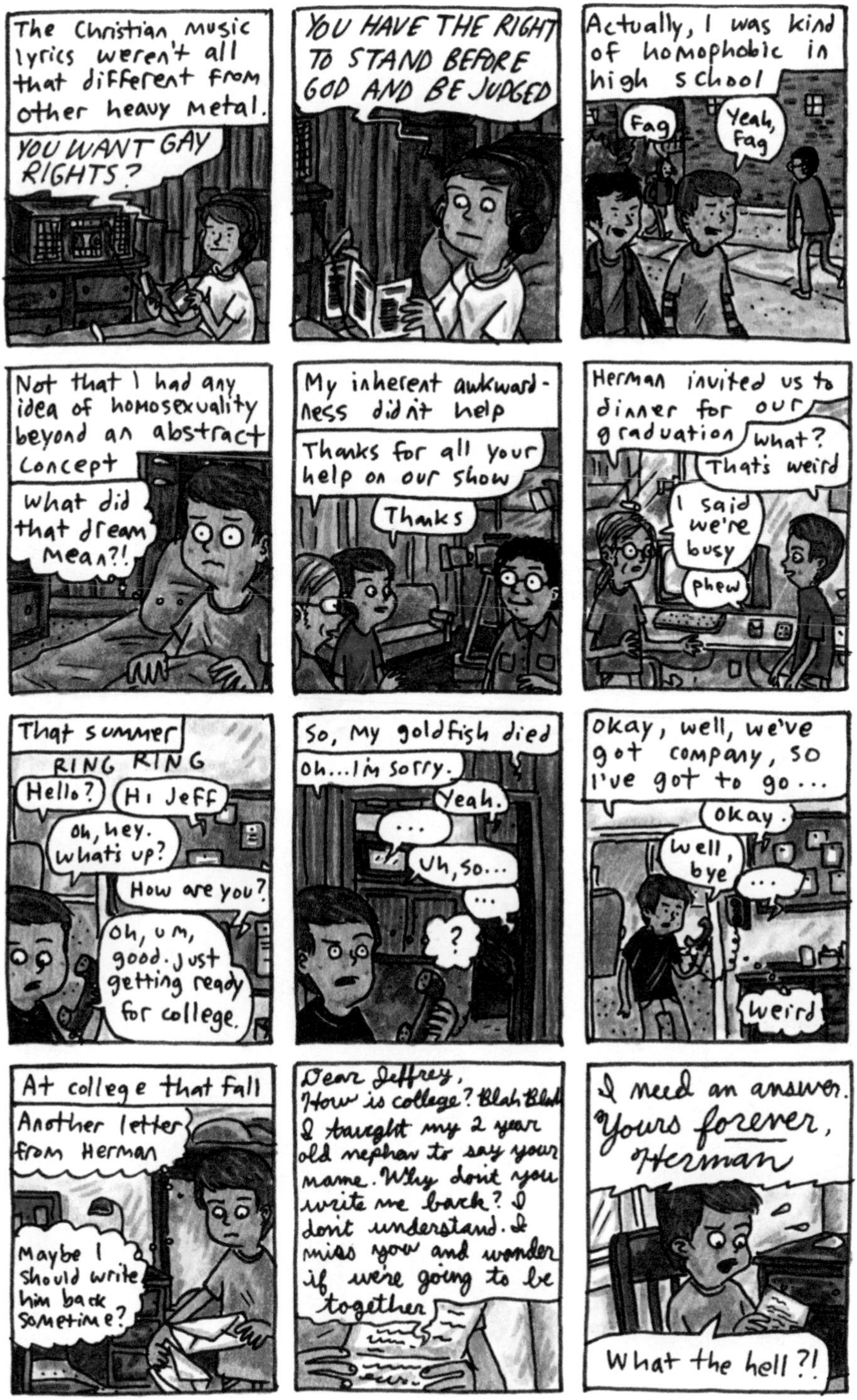
The Christian music lyrics weren't all that different from other heavy metal.
YOU WANT GAY RIGHTS?
YOU HAVE THE RIGHT TO STAND BEFORE GOD AND BE JUDGED
Actually, I was kind of homophobic in high school
Fag
Yeah, Fag
Not that I had any idea of homosexuality beyond an abstract concept
What did that dream mean?!
My inherent awkwardness didn't help
Thanks for all your help on our show
Thanks
Herman invited us to dinner for our graduation
What? That's weird
I said we're busy
phew
That summer
RING RING
Hello?
Hi Jeff
Oh, hey. What's up?
How are you?
Oh, um, good. Just getting ready for college.
So, my goldfish died
Oh... I'm sorry.
Yeah.
...
Uh, so...
...
?
Okay, well, we've got company, so I've got to go...
Okay.
Well, bye
...
Weird
At college that fall
Another letter from Herman
Maybe I should write him back sometime?
Dear Jeffrey, How is college? Blah Blah I taught my 2 year old nephew to say your name. Why don't you write me back? I don't understand. I miss you and wonder if we're going to be together
I need an answer. Yours forever, Herman
What the hell?!

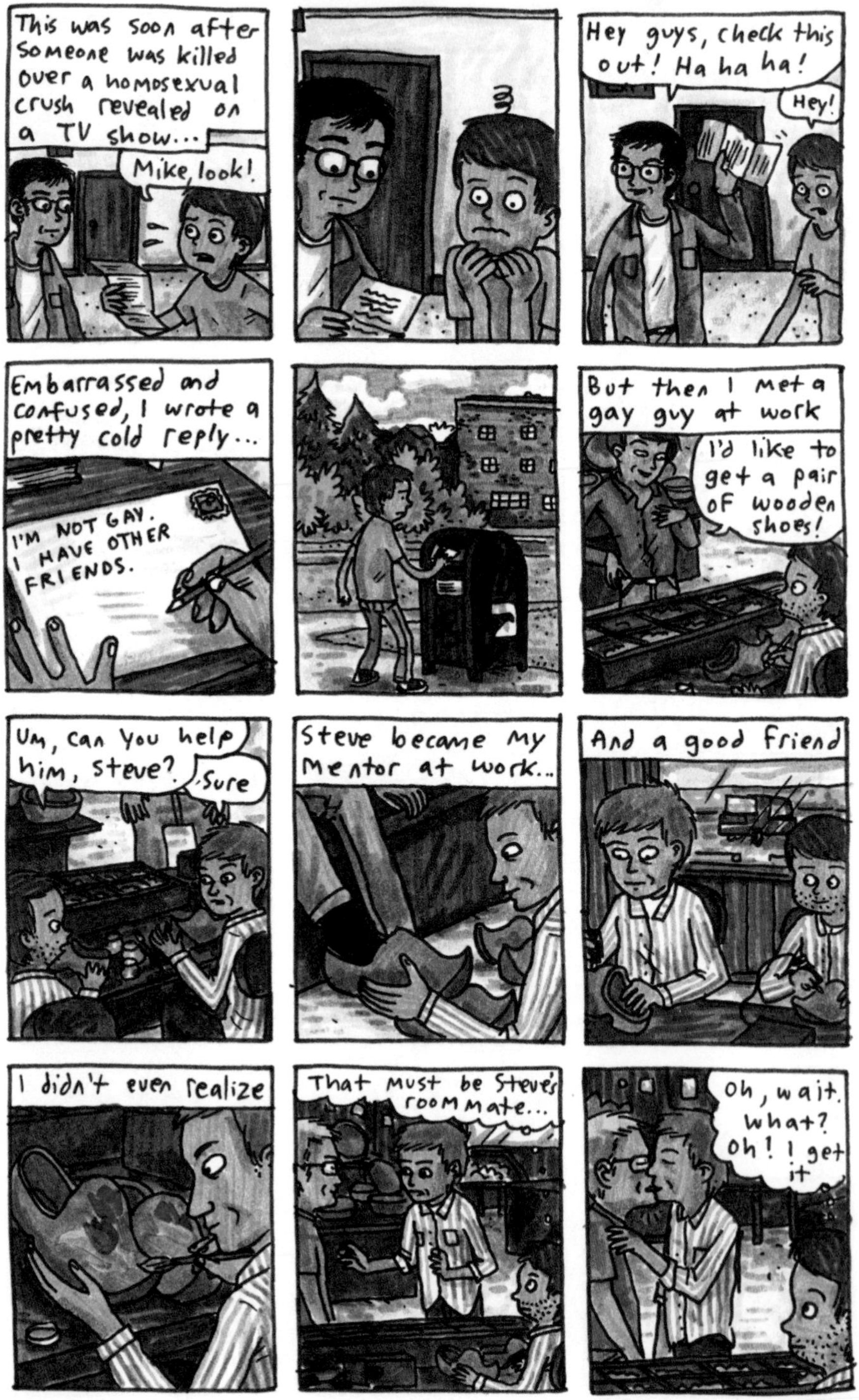
This was soon after someone was killed over a homosexual crush revealed on a TV show...
Mike, look!
Hey guys, check this out! Ha ha ha!
Hey!
Embarrassed and confused, I wrote a pretty cold reply...
I'M NOT GAY. I HAVE OTHER FRIENDS.
But then I met a gay guy at work
I'd like to get a pair of wooden shoes!
Um, can you help him, Steve?
Sure
Steve became my mentor at work...
And a good friend
I didn't even realize
That must be Steve's roommate...
Oh, wait. What? Oh! I get it

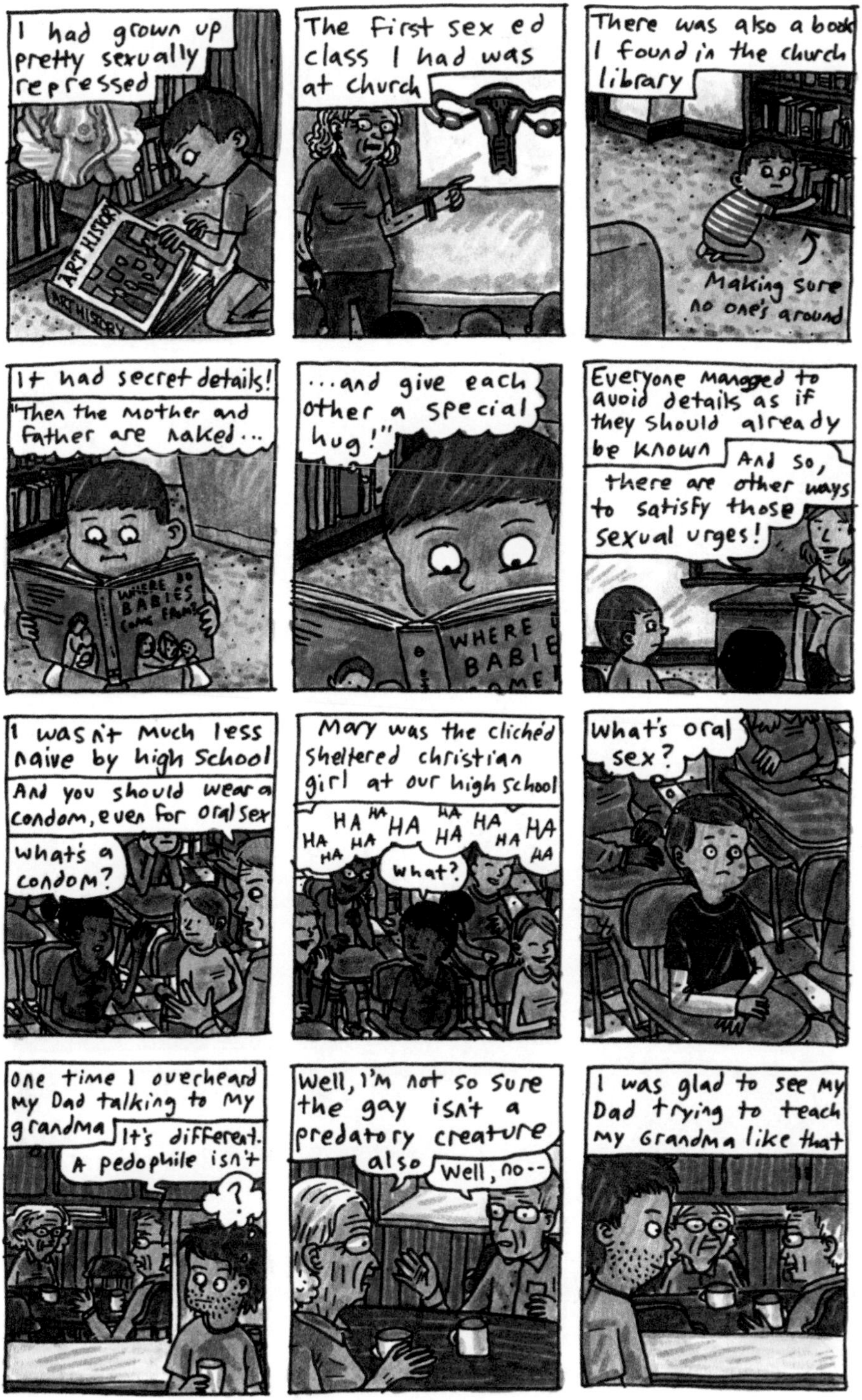
I had grown up pretty sexually repressed
ART HISTORY
The first sex ed class I had was at church
There was also a book I found in the church library
Making sure no one's around
It had secret details!
"Then the mother and father are naked...
...and give each other a special hug!"
WHERE DO BABIES COME FROM?
Everyone managed to avoid details as if they should already be known
And so, there are other ways to satisfy those sexual urges!
I wasn't much less naive by high school
And you should wear a condom, even for oral sex
what's a condom?
Mary was the clichéd sheltered christian girl at our high school
HA HA HA HA HA HA HA HA HA HA HA HA
what?
What's oral sex?
One time I overheard my Dad talking to my grandma
It's different. A pedophile isn't
?
Well, I'm not so sure the gay isn't a predatory creature also
Well, no--
I was glad to see my Dad trying to teach my Grandma like that

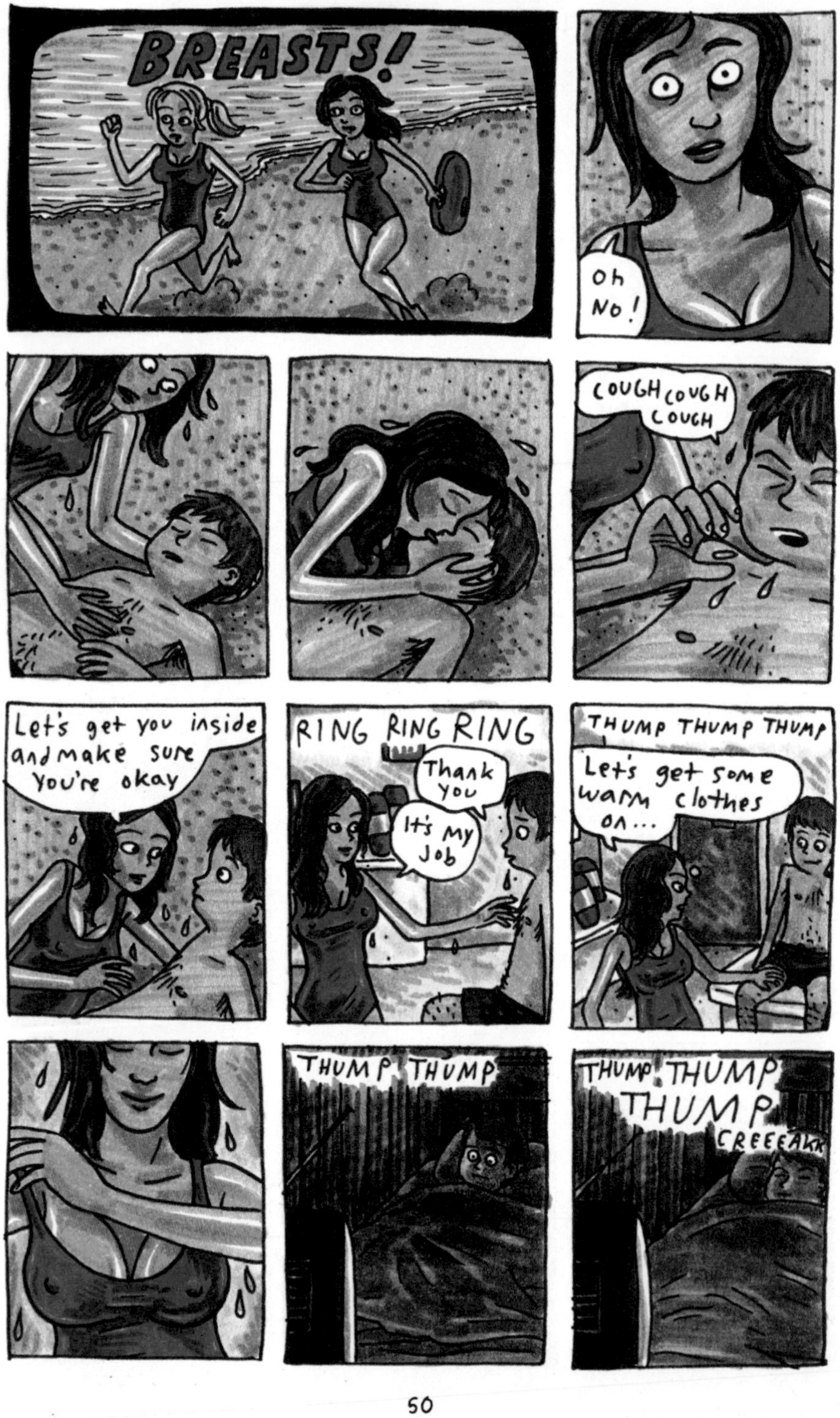
BREASTS!
Oh No!
COUGH COUGH COUGH
Let's get you inside and make sure you're okay
RING RING RING
Thank you
It's my Job
THUMP THUMP THUMP
Let's get some warm clothes on...
THUMP THUMP
THUMP THUMP THUMP
CREEEAKK

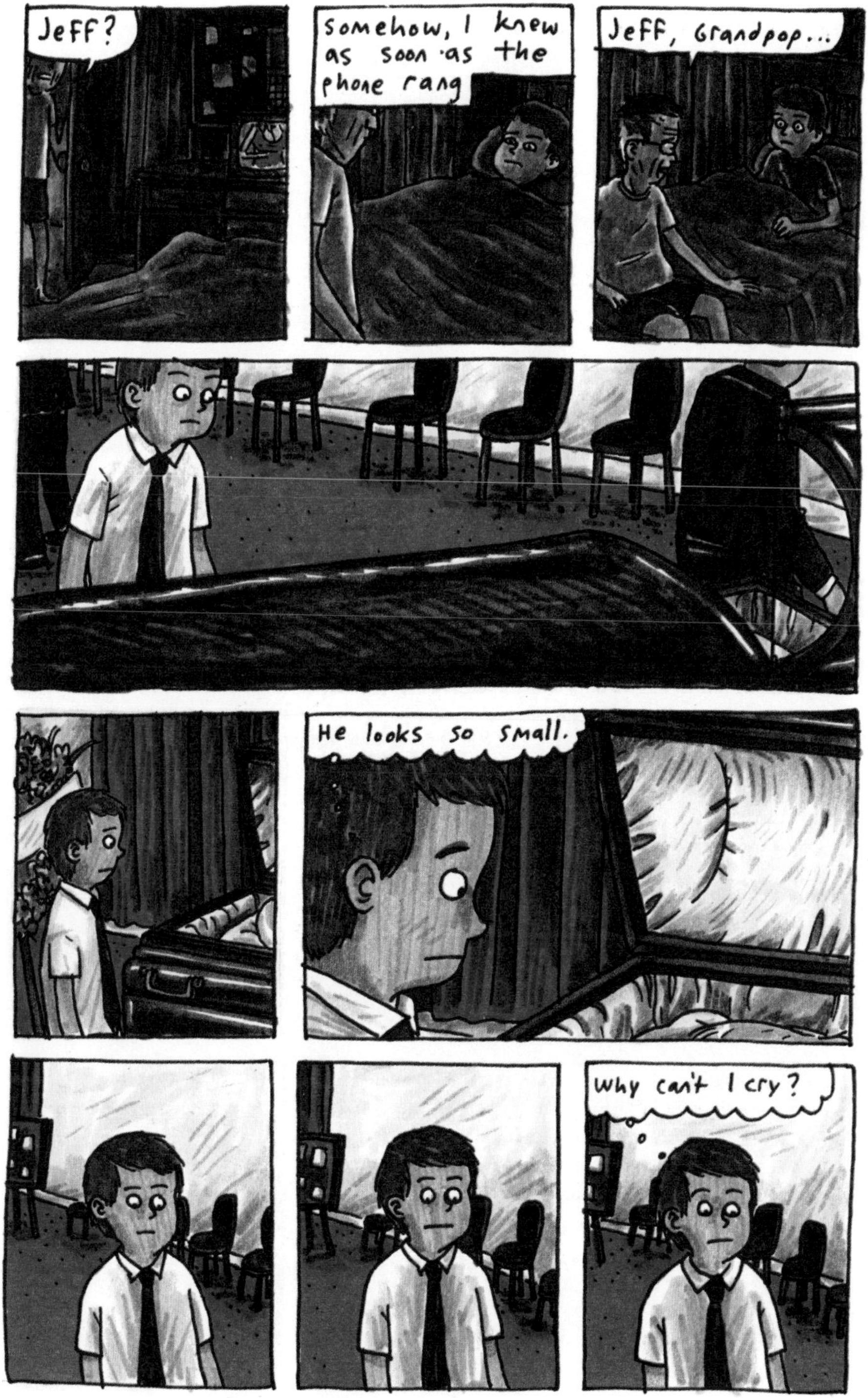
Jeff?
Somehow, I knew as soon as the phone rang
Jeff, Grandpop...
He looks so small.
Why can't I cry?

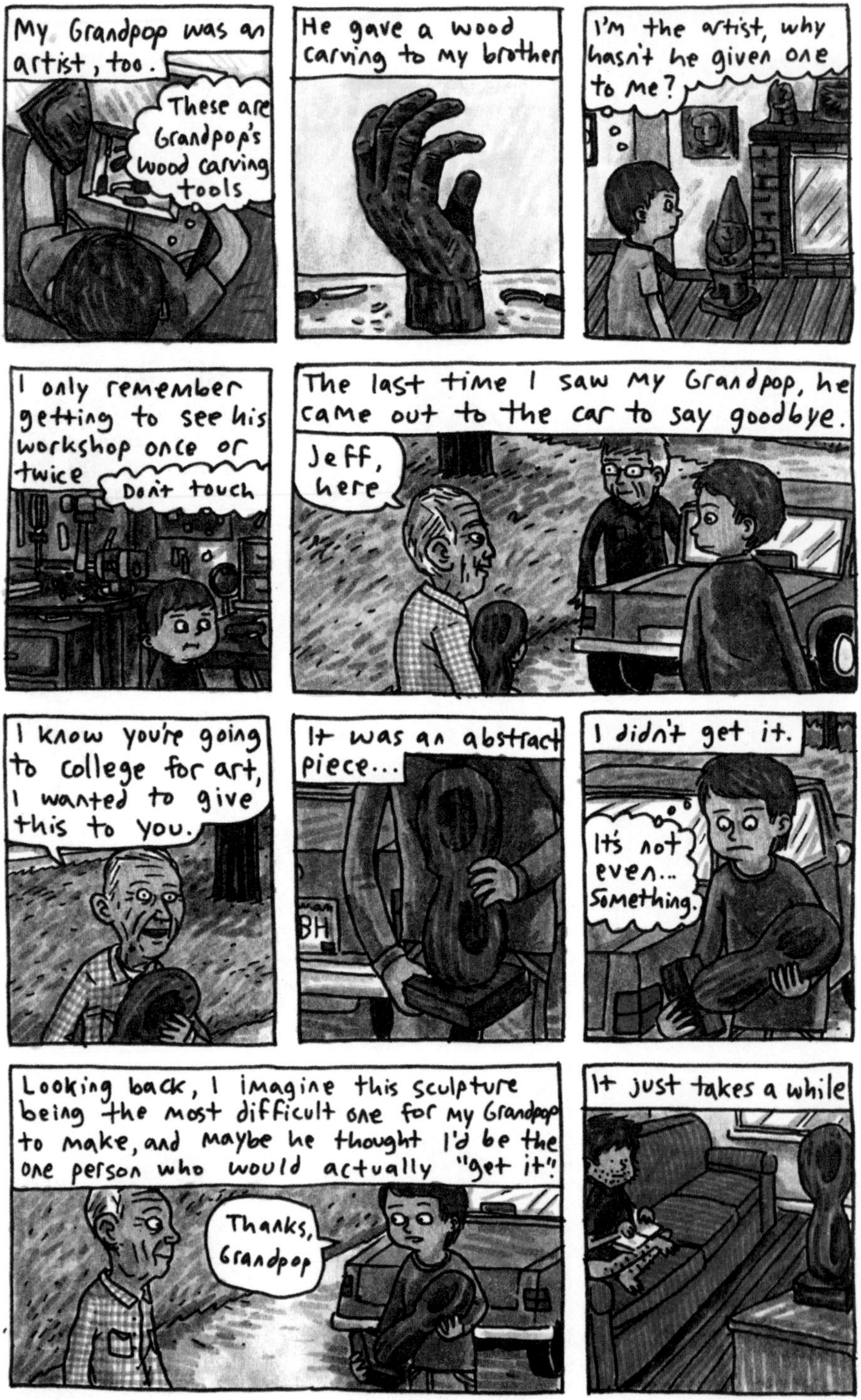
My Grandpop was an artist, too.
These are Grandpop's wood carving tools
He gave a wood carving to my brother
I'm the artist, why hasn't he given one to me?
I only remember getting to see his workshop once or twice
Don't touch
The last time I saw my Grandpop, he came out to the car to say goodbye.
Jeff, here
I know you're going to college for art, I wanted to give this to you.
It was an abstract piece...
I didn't get it.
It's not even... Something.
Looking back, I imagine this sculpture being the most difficult one for my Grandpop to make, and maybe he thought I'd be the one person who would actually "get it".
Thanks, Grandpop
It just takes a while

The Way To God

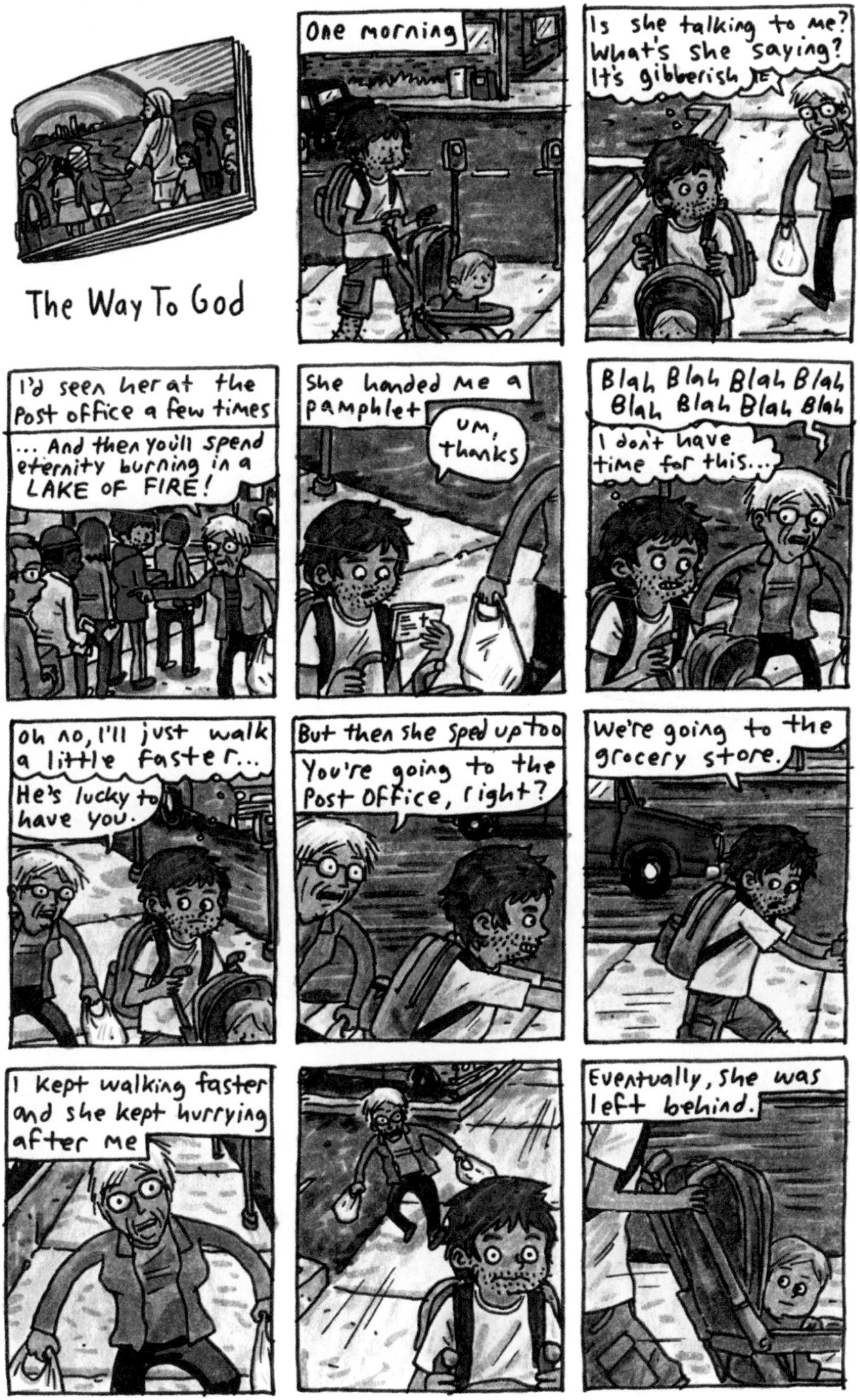

One morning
Is she talking to me? What's she saying? It's gibberish
I'd seen her at the Post office a few times
... And then you'll spend eternity burning in a LAKE OF FIRE!
She handed me a pamphlet
Um, thanks
Blah Blah Blah Blah Blah Blah Blah Blah
I don't have time for this...
oh no, I'll just walk a little faster...
He's lucky to have you.
But then she sped up too
You're going to the Post Office, right?
We're going to the grocery store.
I kept walking faster and she kept hurrying after me
Eventually, she was left behind.

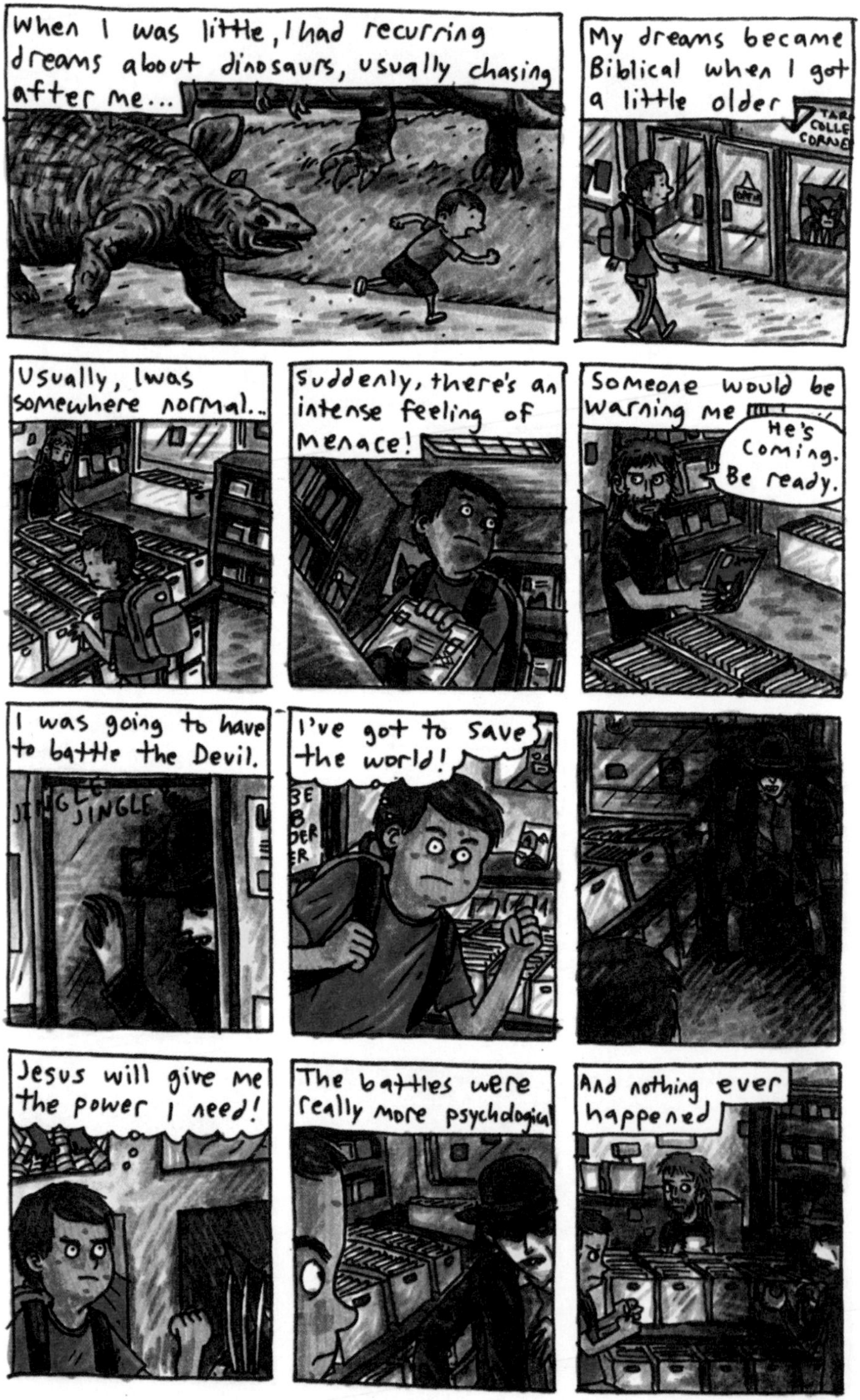
When I was little, I had recurring dreams about dinosaurs, usually chasing after me...
My dreams became Biblical when I got a little older
Usually, I was somewhere normal...
Suddenly, there's an intense feeling of menace!
Someone would be warning me
He's coming. Be ready.
I was going to have to battle the Devil.
JINGLE JINGLE
I've got to save the world!
Jesus will give me the power I need!
The battles were really more psychological
And nothing ever happened

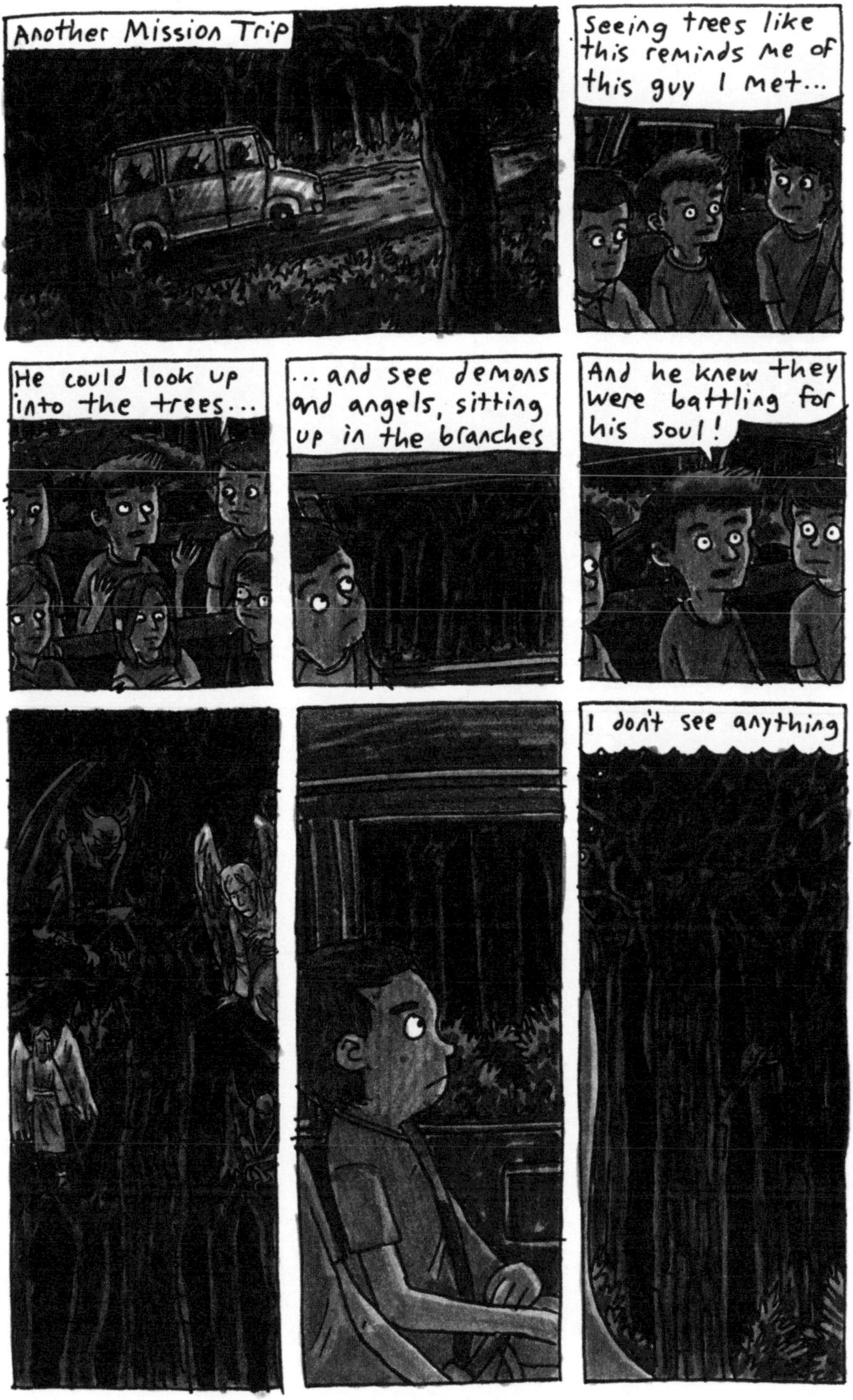

Another Mission Trip
Seeing trees like this reminds me of this guy I met...
He could look up into the trees...
...and see demons and angels, sitting up in the branches
And he knew they were battling for his soul!
I don't see anything

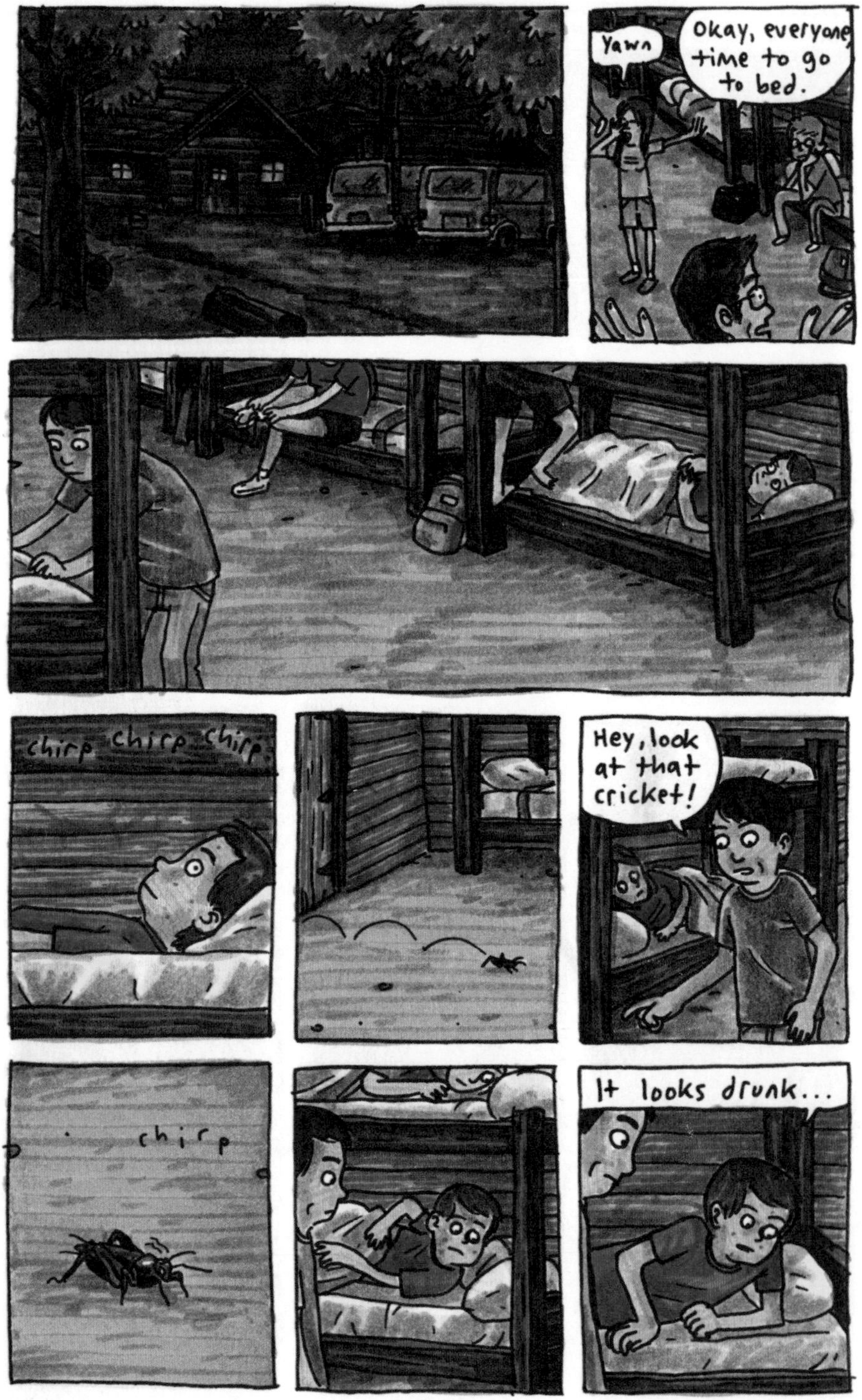
Yawn
Okay, everyone, time to go to bed.
chirp chirp chirp
Hey, look at that cricket!
chirp
It looks drunk...

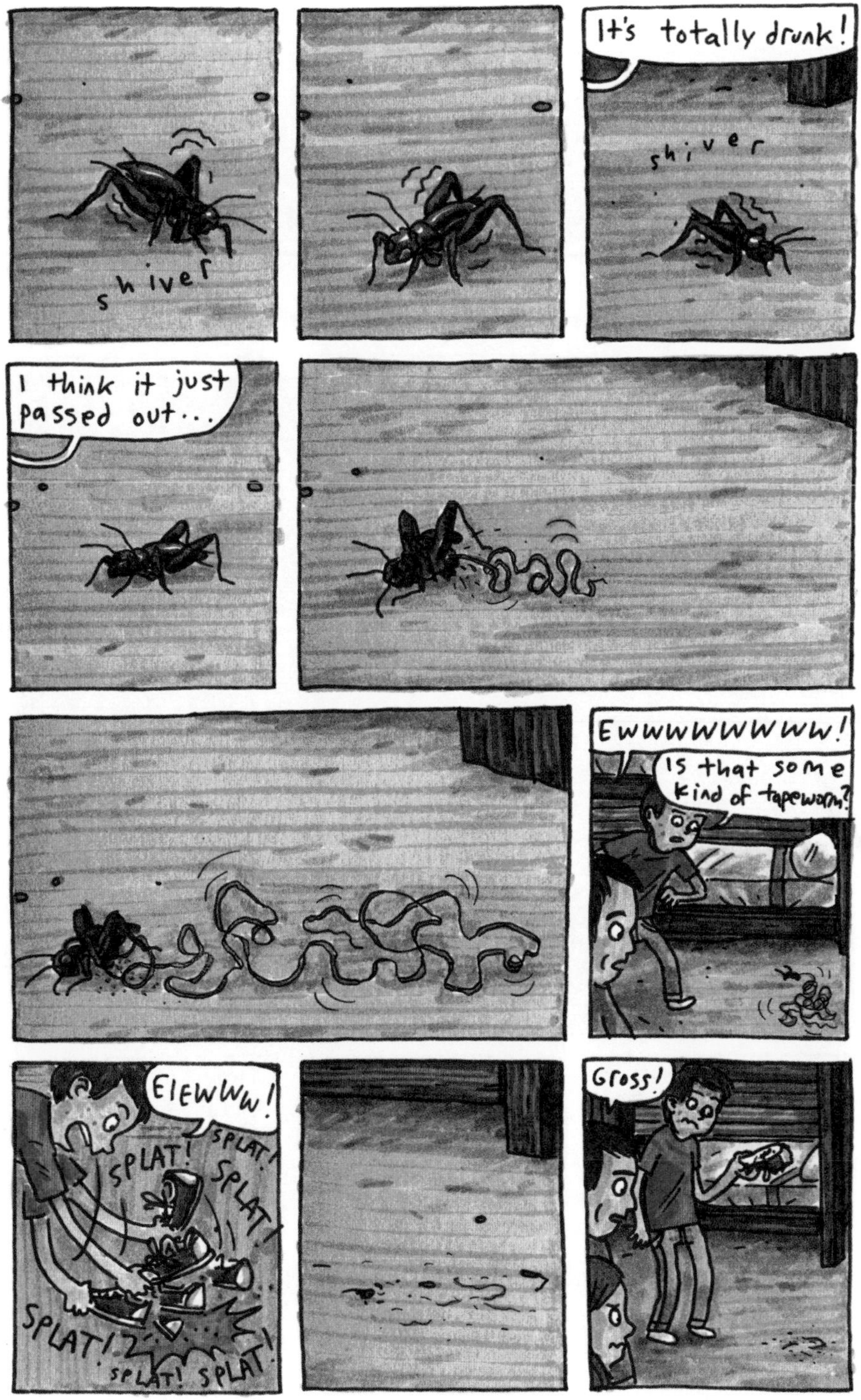

shiver
It's totally drunk!
shiver
I think it just passed out...
EWWWWWWWW!
Is that some kind of tapeworm?
EIEWWW!
SPLAT!
SPLAT!
SPLAT!
SPLAT!
SPLAT!
SPLAT!
SPLAT!
Gross!

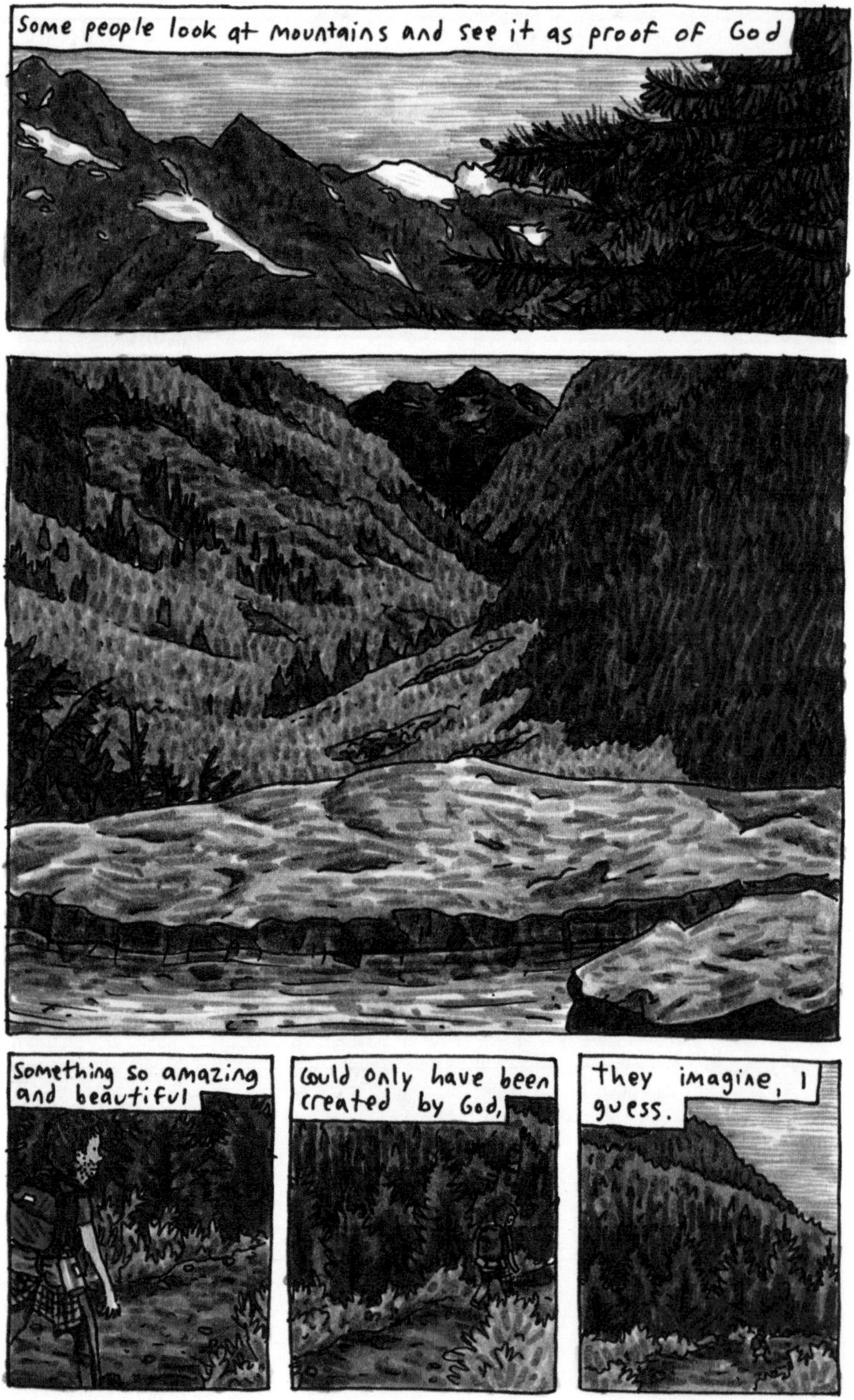
Some people look at mountains and see it as proof of God
Something so amazing and beautiful
could only have been created by God,
they imagine, I guess.

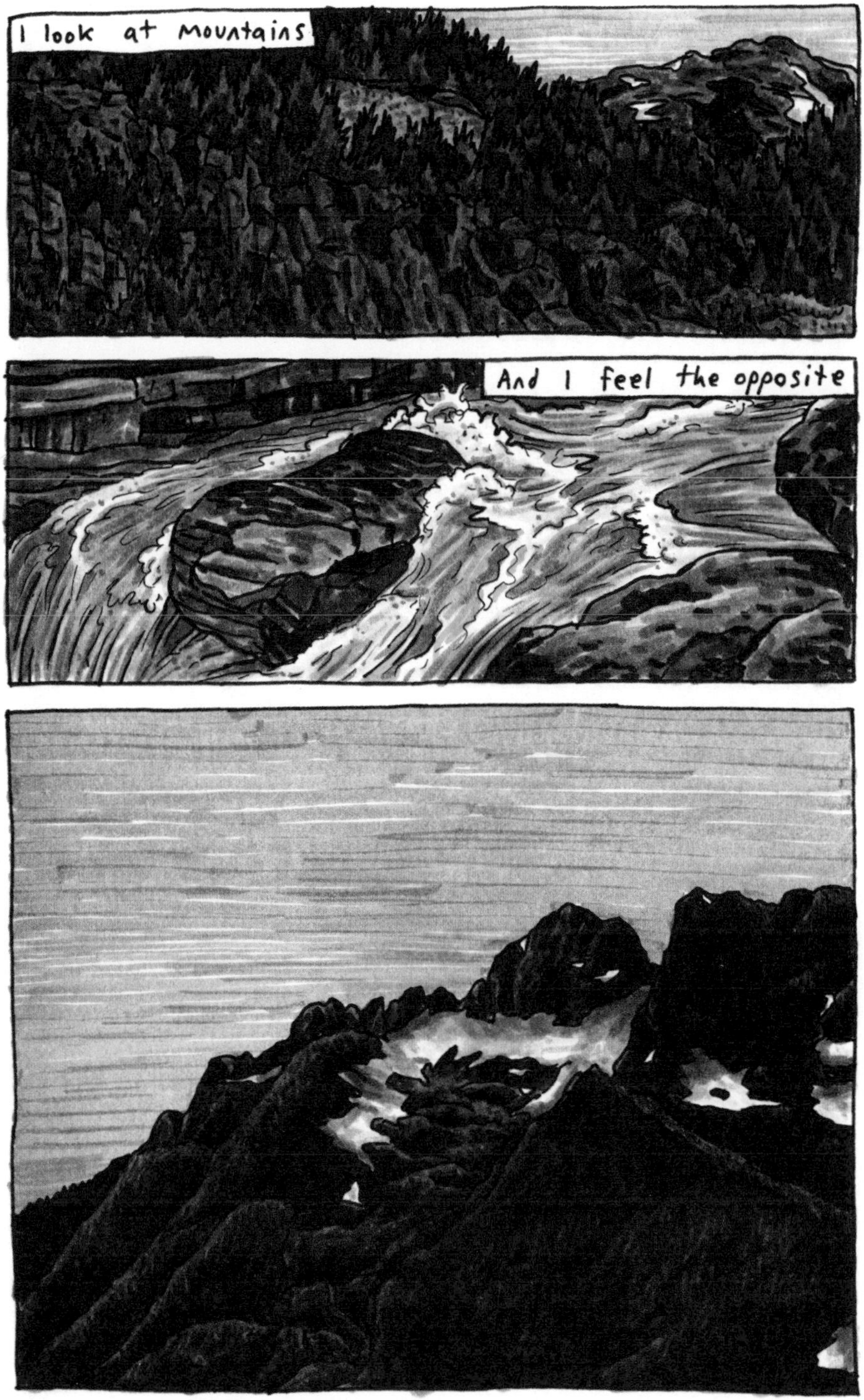
I look at mountains
And I feel the opposite

My digestive problems began when I was young

Please God, help me get this out!

If you do I'll be good for Mom and Dad

I love you, Mom

Um, I clogged the toilet upstairs.

I had surgery in high school, and by the time I finished college I was feeling better

Jeffrey?

Mostly

So, Jeff, how have you been feeling?

Okay, but I've been having a lot of discomfort off and on

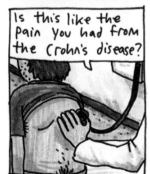

Is this like the pain you had from the Crohn's disease?

No, it's different... just a lot of upset stomach stuff. And just...irregular.

What else is going on in your life? Have you been stressed a lot lately?

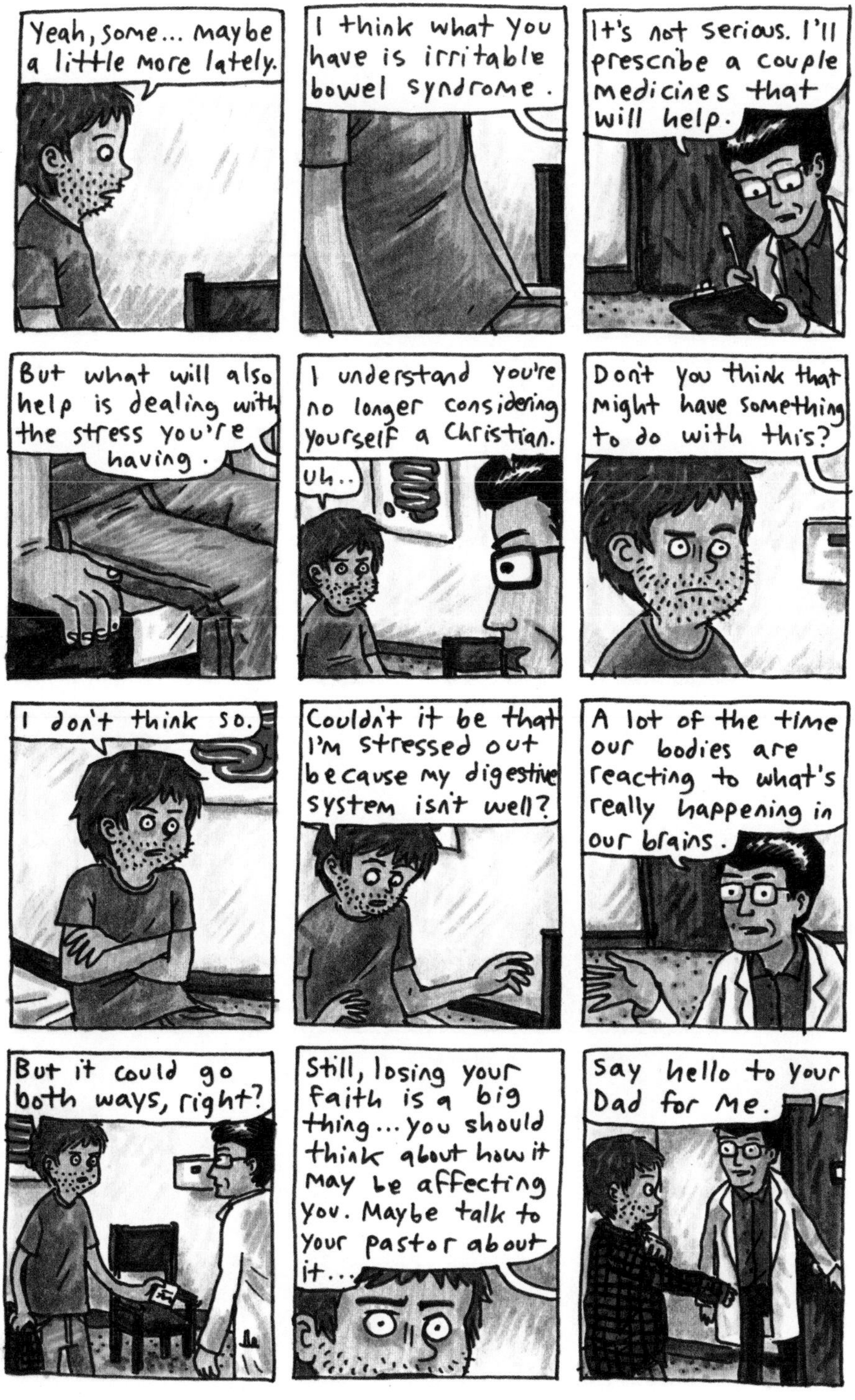
Yeah, some... maybe a little more lately.
I think what you have is irritable bowel syndrome.
It's not serious. I'll prescribe a couple medicines that will help.
But what will also help is dealing with the stress you're having.
I understand you're no longer considering yourself a Christian.
Uh..
Don't you think that might have something to do with this?
I don't think so.
Couldn't it be that I'm stressed out because my digestive system isn't well?
A lot of the time our bodies are reacting to what's really happening in our brains.
But it could go both ways, right?
Still, losing your faith is a big thing... you should think about how it may be affecting you. Maybe talk to your pastor about it...
Say hello to your Dad for me.

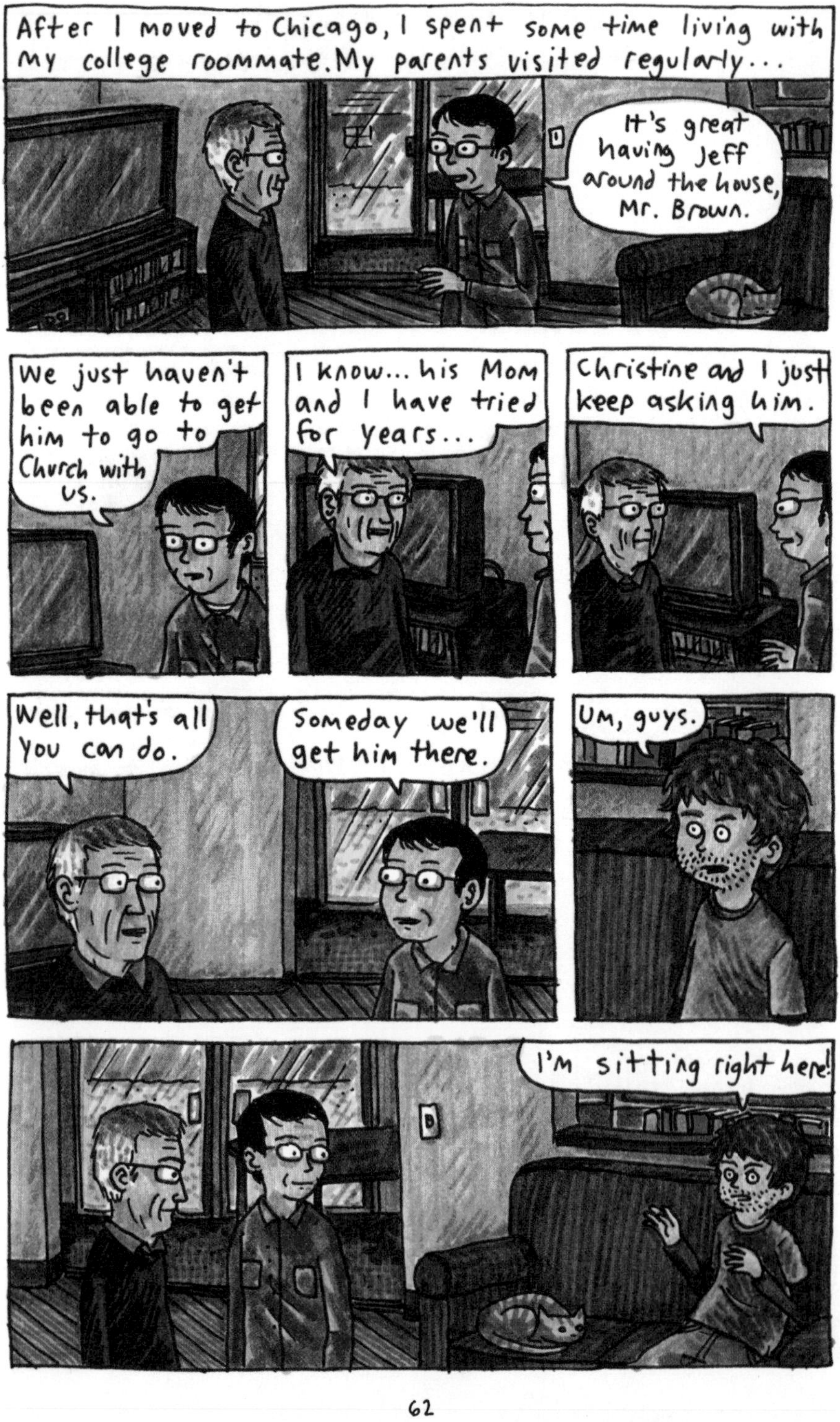
After I moved to Chicago, I spent some time living with my college roommate. My parents visited regularly...
It's great having Jeff around the house, Mr. Brown.
We just haven't been able to get him to go to Church with us.
I know... his Mom and I have tried for years...
Christine and I just keep asking him.
Well, that's all you can do.
Someday we'll get him there.
Um, guys.
I'm sitting right here!

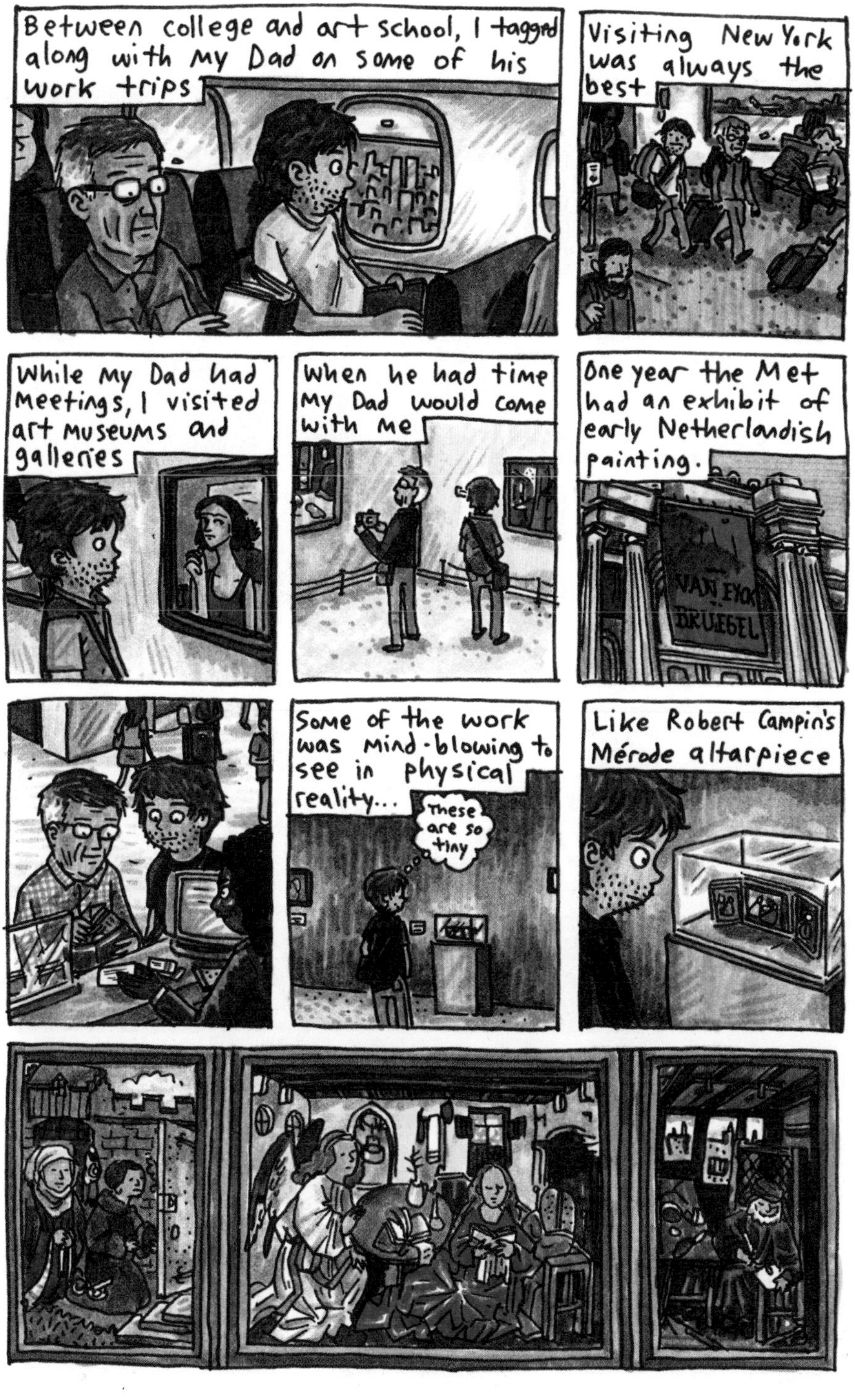
Between college and art school, I tagged along with my Dad on some of his work trips
Visiting New York was always the best
While my Dad had meetings, I visited art museums and galleries
When he had time my Dad would come with me
One year the Met had an exhibit of early Netherlandish painting.
VAN EYCK
BRUEGEL
Some of the work was mind-blowing to see in physical reality...
These are so tiny
Like Robert Campin's Mérode altarpiece

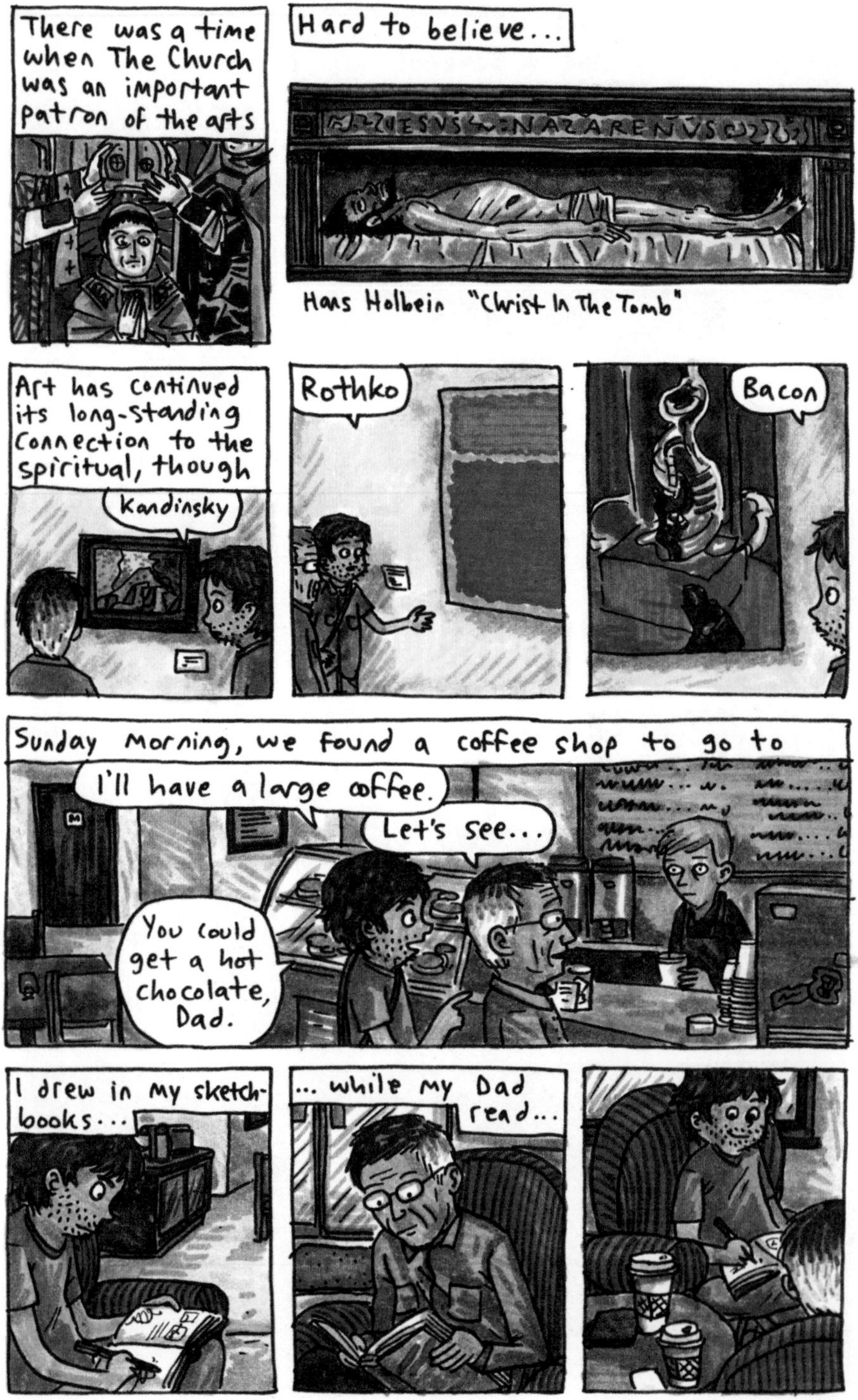
There was a time when The Church was an important patron of the arts
Hard to believe...
IESVS NAZARENVS
Hans Holbein "Christ In The Tomb"
Art has continued its long-standing connection to the spiritual, though
Kandinsky
Rothko
Bacon
Sunday morning, we found a coffee shop to go to
I'll have a large coffee.
Let's see...
You could get a hot chocolate, Dad.
I drew in my sketch-books...
... while my Dad read...

Not quite ten years later, I was in London

I was looking at art, alone this time.

Jennifer and Oscar were supposed to be there with me already

Jenny Holzer

If they had been, I probably wouldn't have been at the Tate Museum looking at art.

SOME DAYS YOU WAKE AND IMMEDIATELY START TO WORRY, NOTHING IN PARTICULAR IS WRONG, IT'S JUST THE SUSPICION THAT FORCES ARE ALIGNING QUIETLY AND THERE WILL BE TROUBLE.

Ha

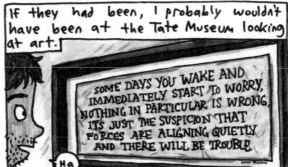

One week earlier... I got our passports out.

Already?

I want to make sure they're valid.

Let's see, mine's good, Oscar's, yep... yours...

Oh shit!

Uhhhhh

You're joking, right?

Oh shit.

How is this possible?! I just got this last year! Probably because it was a replacement for the stolen one.

What are we going to do? I can't stay here with this baby while you're gone for two weeks! There's got to be some way...

Look, there's emergency passport services you can use... Are they legit? I hope so.

Okay, you make dinner, I'll start calling...

Dangit!

Okay, I called and they can do it, but we still have to change my flight and Oscar's... Crap! spill

Talk to an operator... change tickets... previously booked... Change... Talk to an operator Beep Beep Beep Operator. I'm sorry G#*#*! automated system Beep

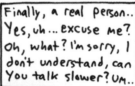

Finally, a real person.. Yes, uh...excuse me? Oh, what? I'm sorry, I don't understand, can you talk slower? Um.. Could I talk to someone else?

Um, yes... Sorry, no offense, I just couldn't understand anything she was saying.

Okay, I got the flights fixed. You just need to give them your credit card at the check in desk at the airport. Okay

The passport guy emailed... he'll call me tomorrow and let me know where to FedEx my stuff... Good.

I'm going to repack in case you end up not making it. You think I won't make it? You'll make it.

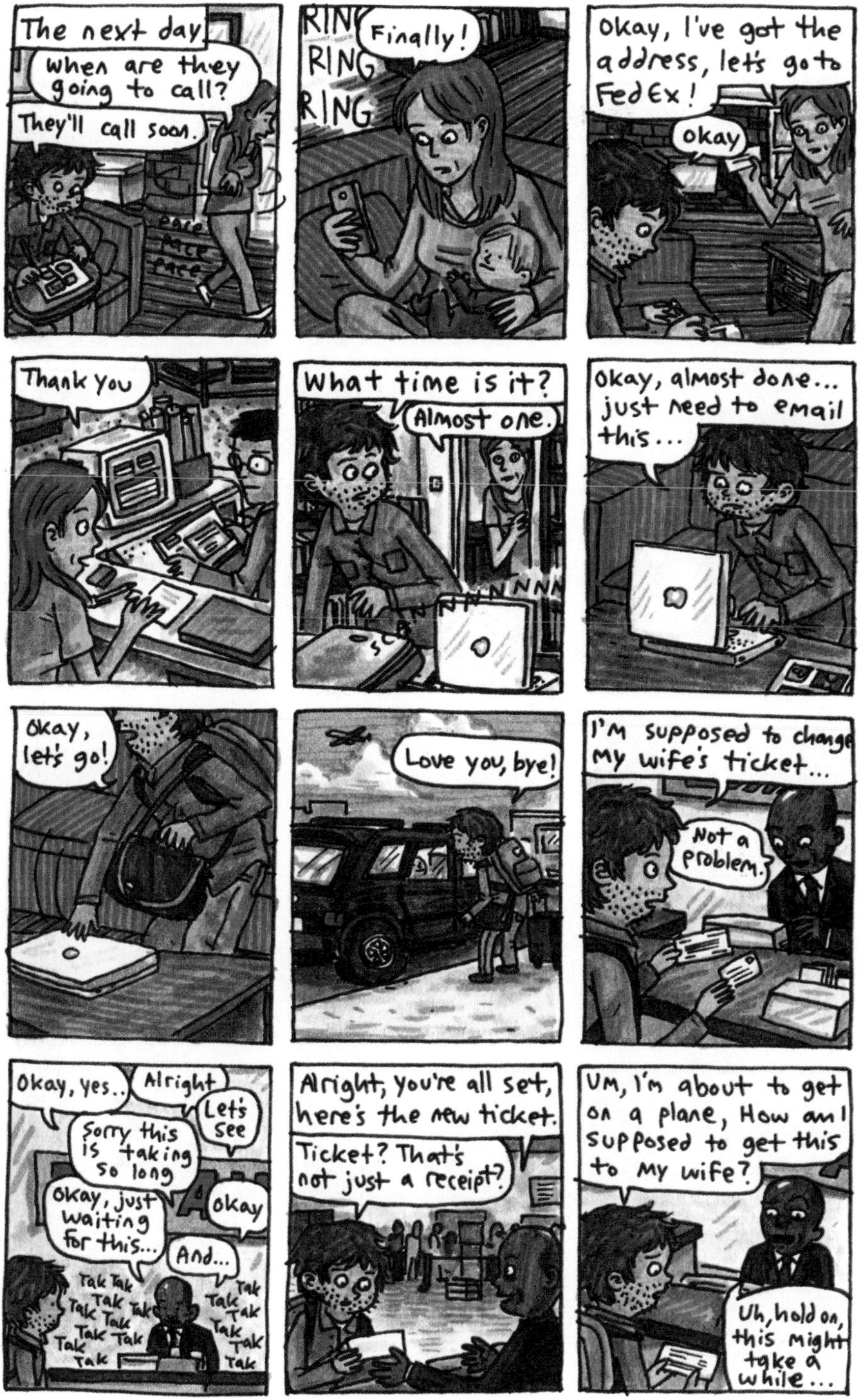
The next day
When are they going to call?
They'll call soon.
Pace Pace Pace
RING RING RING
Finally!
Okay, I've got the address, let's go to FedEx!
Okay
Thank you
What time is it?
Almost one.
Okay, almost done... just need to email this...
Okay, let's go!
Love you, bye!
I'm supposed to change my wife's ticket...
Not a problem.
Okay, yes..
Alright
Let's see
Sorry this is taking so long
Okay, just waiting for this...
Okay
And...
Tak Tak Tak Tak Tak Tak Tak Tak Tak Tak Tak Tak Tak Tak Tak Tak Tak
Alright, you're all set, here's the new ticket.
Ticket? That's not just a receipt?
Um, I'm about to get on a plane, How am I supposed to get this to my wife?
Uh, hold on, this might take a while...

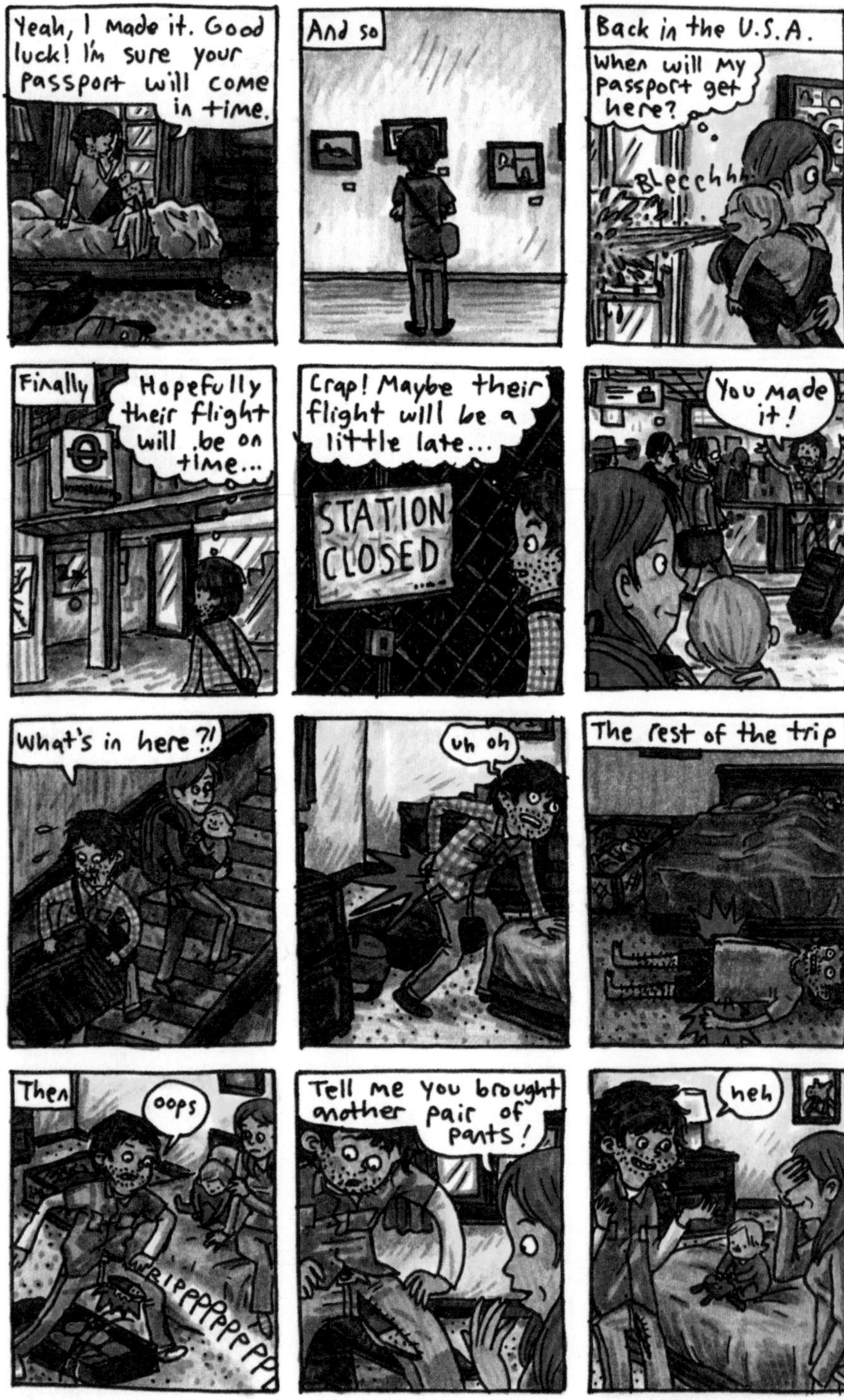
Yeah, I made it. Good luck! I'm sure your passport will come in time.
And so
Back in the U.S.A.
When will my passport get here?
Blecchh
Finally
Hopefully their flight will be on time...
Crap! Maybe their flight will be a little late...
STATION CLOSED
You made it!
What's in here?!
uh oh
The rest of the trip
Then
oops
RIPPPPPPPPP
Tell me you brought another pair of pants!
heh

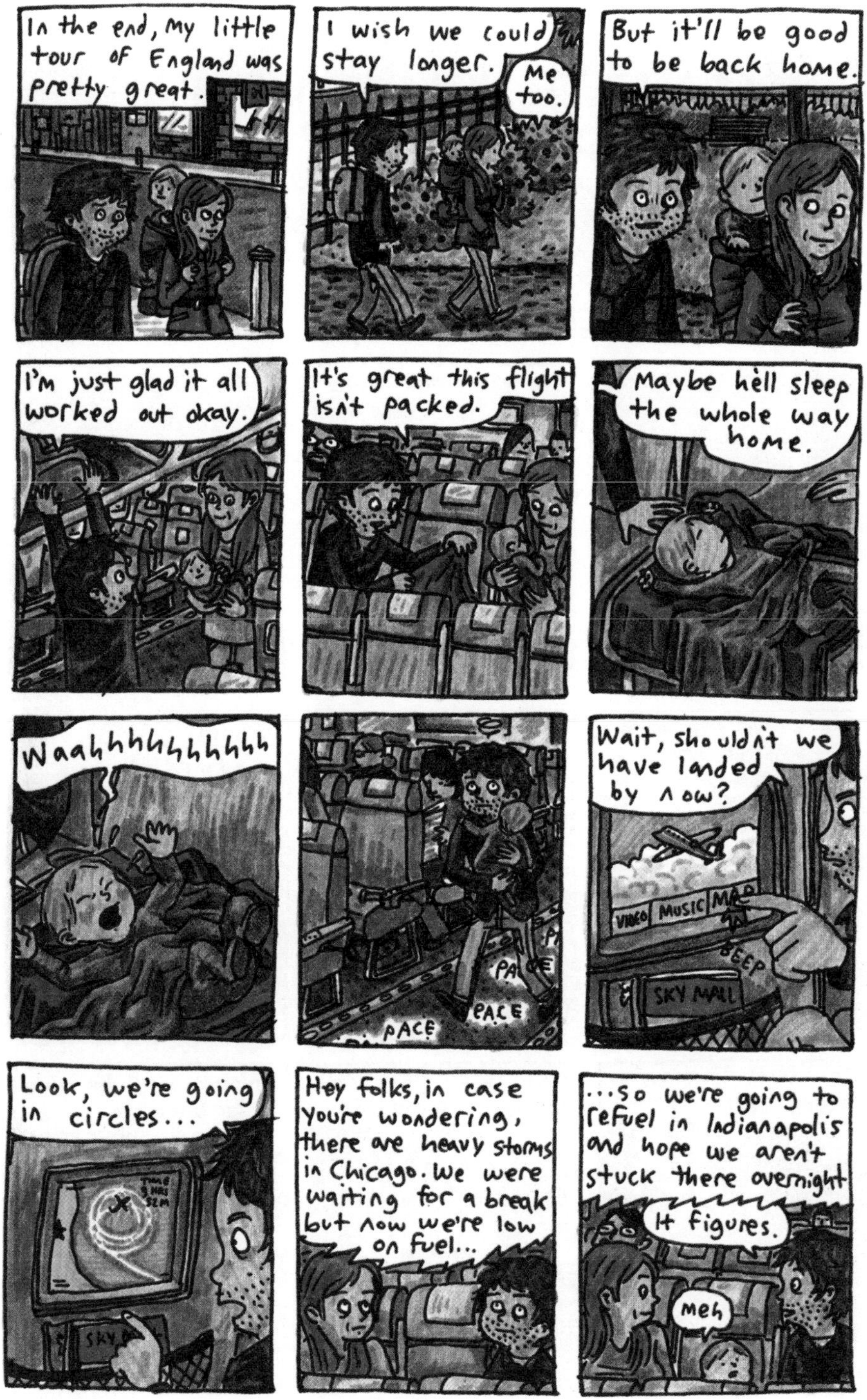
In the end, my little tour of England was pretty great.
I wish we could stay longer.
Me too.
But it'll be good to be back home.
I'm just glad it all worked out okay.
It's great this flight isn't packed.
Maybe he'll sleep the whole way home.
Waahhhhhhhhhh
PACE
PACE
PACE
Wait, shouldn't we have landed by now?
VIDEO
MUSIC
BEEP
SKY MALL
Look, we're going in circles...
Hey folks, in case you're wondering, there are heavy storms in Chicago. We were waiting for a break but now we're low on fuel...
...so we're going to refuel in Indianapolis and hope we aren't stuck there overnight
It figures.
meh

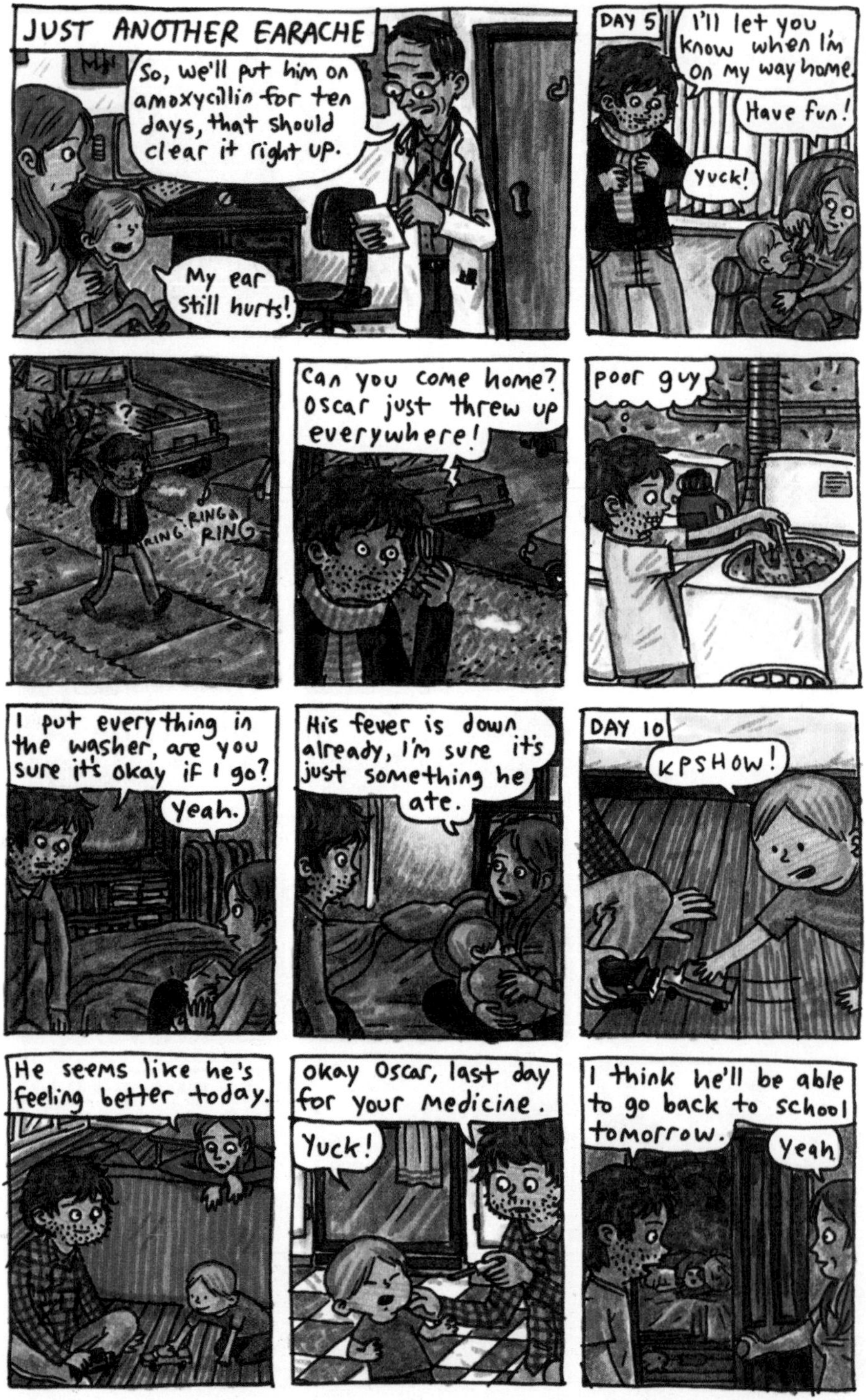
JUST ANOTHER EARACHE
So, we'll put him on amoxycillin for ten days, that should clear it right up.
My ear still hurts!
DAY 5
I'll let you know when I'm on my way home.
Have fun!
Yuck!
?
RING RING RING
Can you come home? Oscar just threw up everywhere!
poor guy
I put everything in the washer, are you sure it's okay if I go?
Yeah.
His fever is down already, I'm sure it's just something he ate.
DAY 10
KPSHOW!
He seems like he's feeling better today.
Okay Oscar, last day for your medicine.
Yuck!
I think he'll be able to go back to school tomorrow.
Yeah

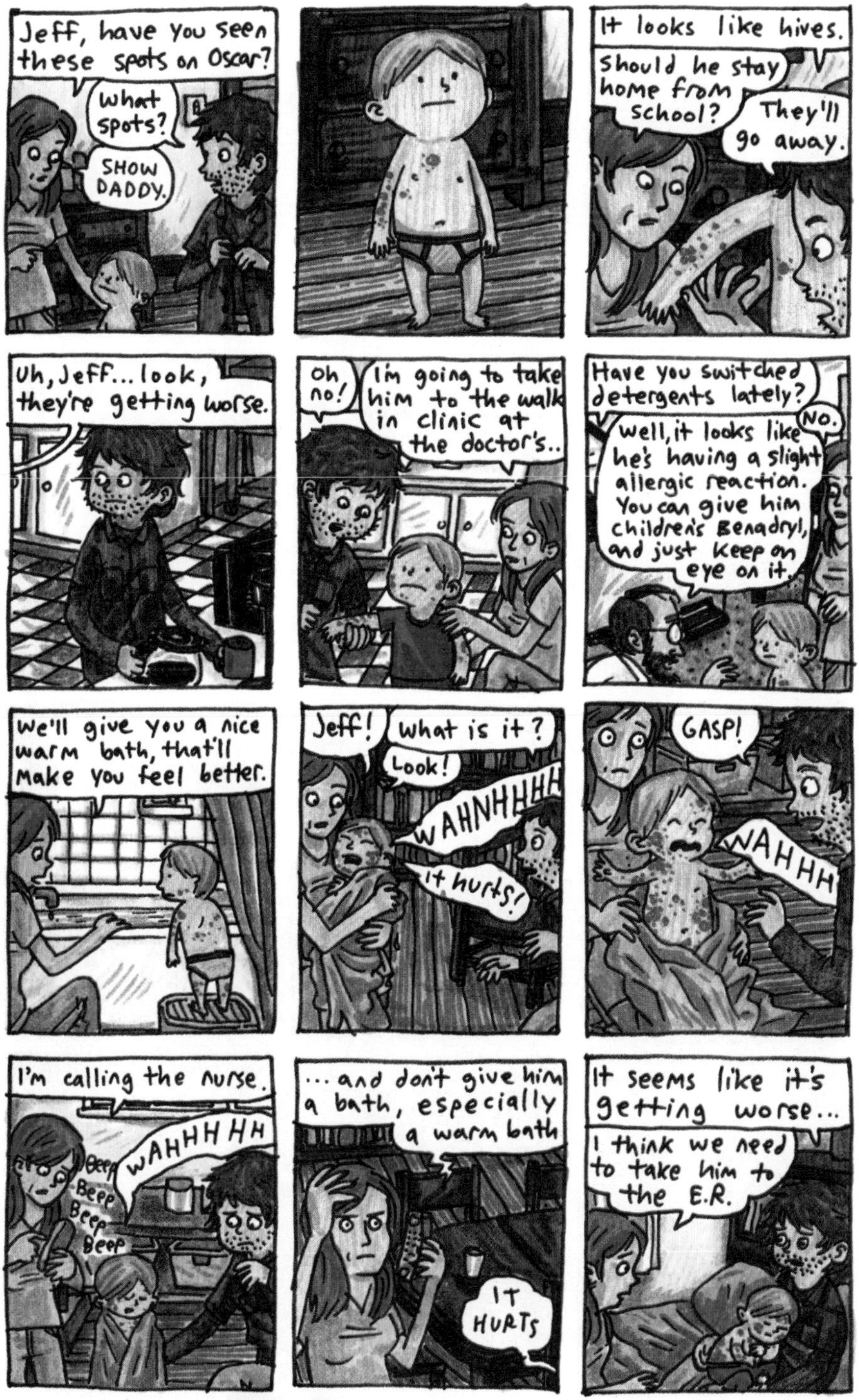
Jeff, have you seen these spots on Oscar?
What spots?
SHOW DADDY.
It looks like hives.
Should he stay home from school?
They'll go away.
Uh, Jeff... look, they're getting worse.
Oh no!
I'm going to take him to the walk in clinic at the doctor's..
Have you switched detergents lately?
NO.
Well, it looks like he's having a slight allergic reaction. You can give him children's Benadryl, and just keep an eye on it.
We'll give you a nice warm bath, that'll make you feel better.
Jeff!
What is it?
Look!
WAHNHHHH
it hurts!
GASP!
WAHHHH
I'm calling the nurse.
WAHHHHHH
Beep
Beep
Beep
Beep
...and don't give him a bath, especially a warm bath
IT HURTS
It seems like it's getting worse...
I think we need to take him to the E.R.

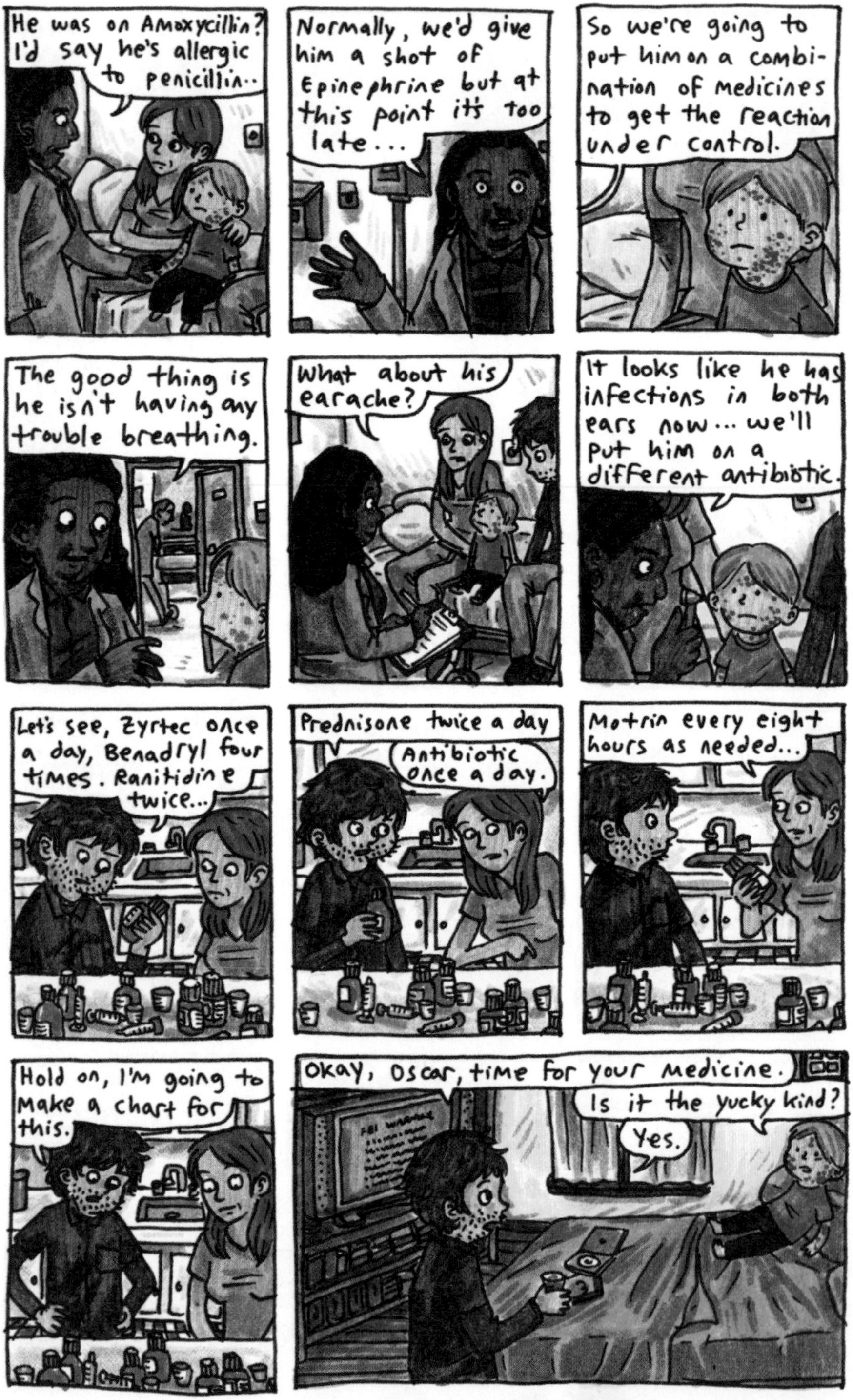
He was on Amoxycillin? I'd say he's allergic to penicillin..
Normally, we'd give him a shot of Epinephrine but at this point it's too late...
So we're going to put him on a combination of medicines to get the reaction under control.
The good thing is he isn't having any trouble breathing.
What about his earache?
It looks like he has infections in both ears now... we'll put him on a different antibiotic.
Let's see, Zyrtec once a day, Benadryl four times. Ranitidine twice...
Prednisone twice a day
Antibiotic once a day.
Motrin every eight hours as needed...
Hold on, I'm going to make a chart for this.
Okay, Oscar, time for your medicine.
Is it the yucky kind?
Yes.

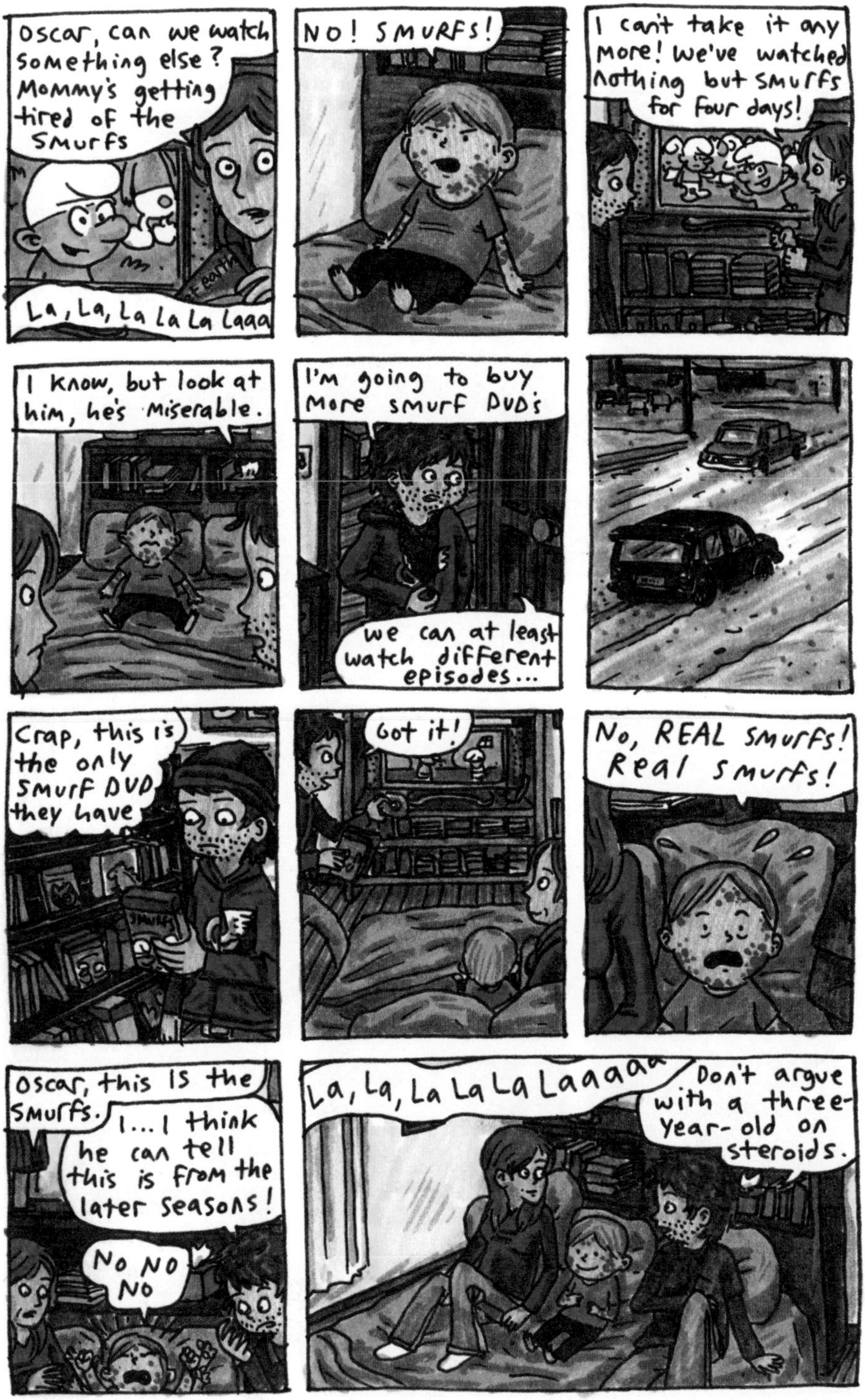
Oscar, can we watch something else? Mommy's getting tired of the Smurfs
La, La, La La La Laaa
NO! SMURFS!
I can't take it any more! We've watched nothing but smurfs for four days!
I know, but look at him, he's miserable.
I'm going to buy more smurf DVD's
we can at least watch different episodes...
Crap, this is the only smurf DVD they have
Got it!
No, REAL smurfs! Real smurfs!
Oscar, this IS the smurfs.
I... I think he can tell this is from the later seasons!
NO NO NO
La, La, La La La Laaaaa
Don't argue with a three-year-old on steroids.

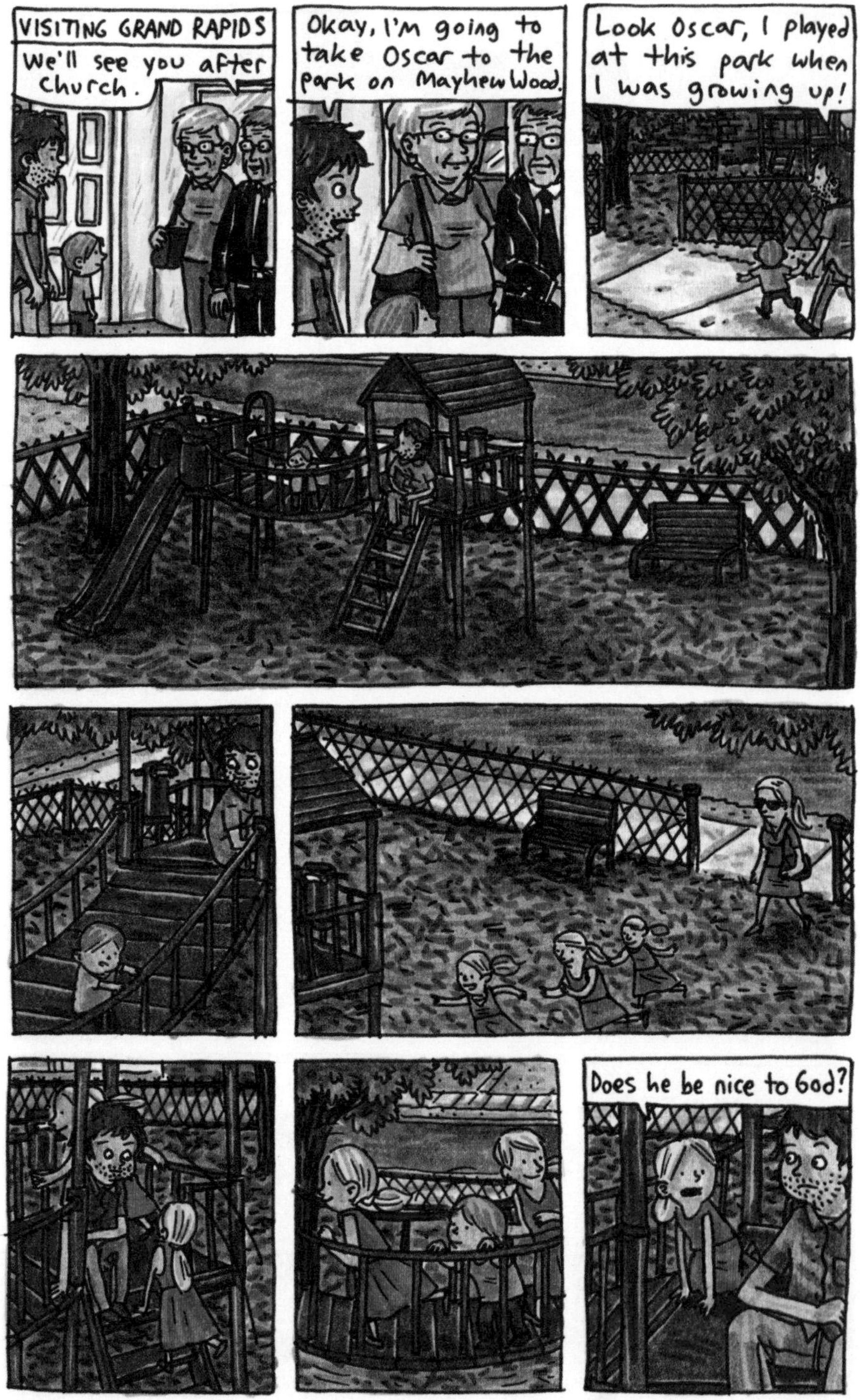
VISITING GRAND RAPIDS
We'll see you after church.
Okay, I'm going to take Oscar to the park on Mayhew Wood.
Look Oscar, I played at this park when I was growing up!
Does he be nice to God?

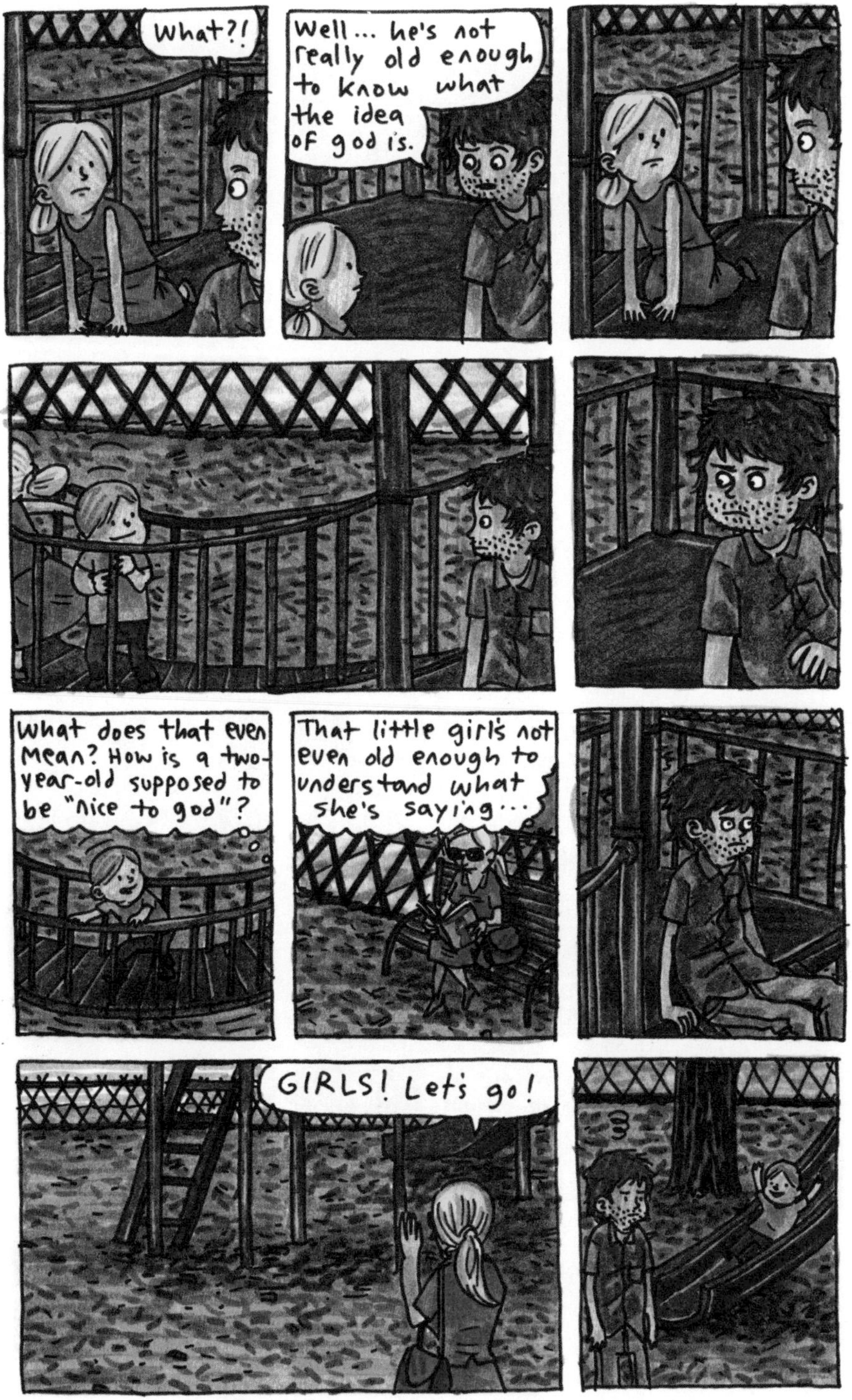
What?!
Well... he's not really old enough to know what the idea of god is.
What does that even Mean? How is a two-year-old supposed to be "nice to god"?
That little girl's not even old enough to understand what she's saying...
GIRLS! Let's go!

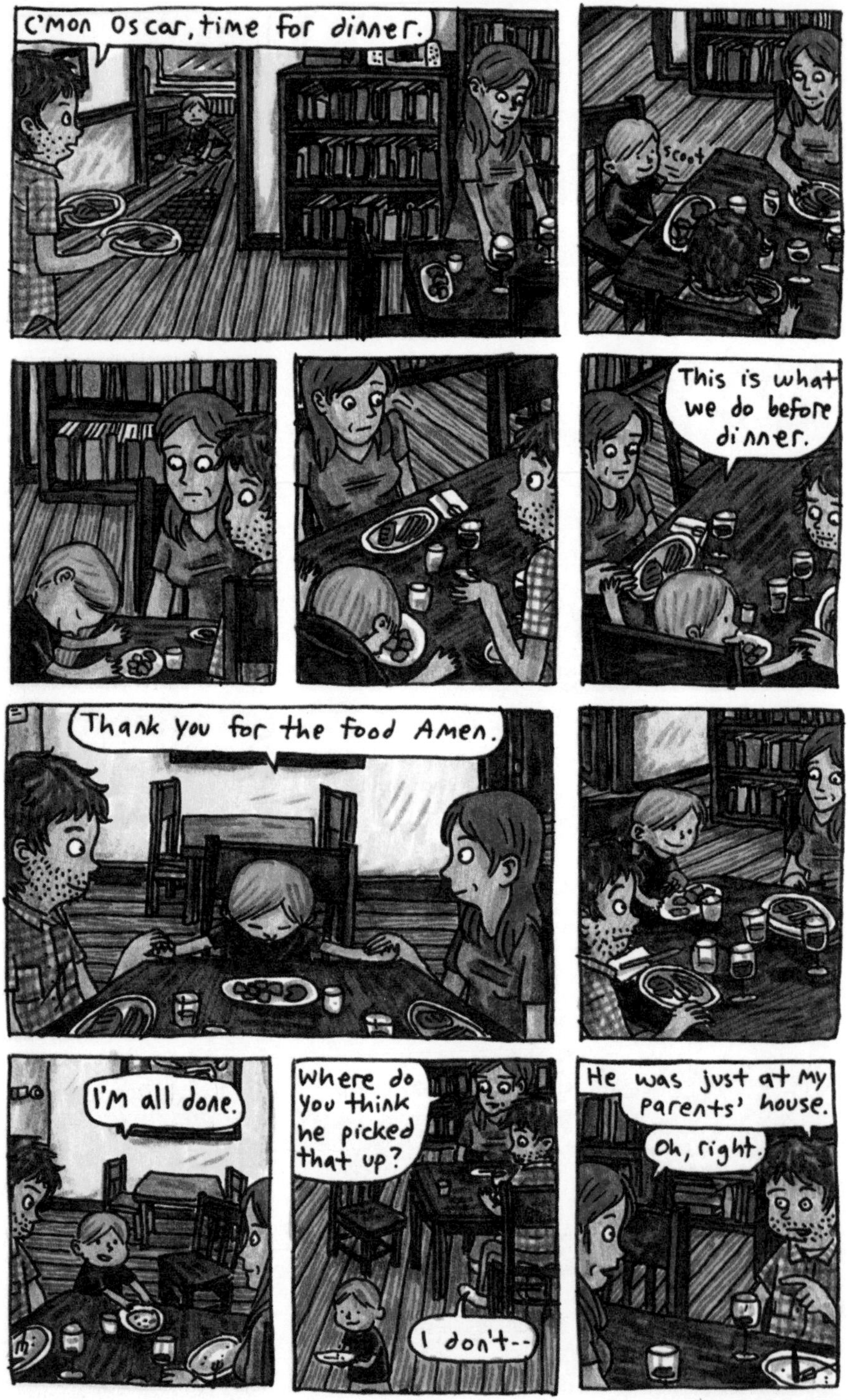
C'mon Oscar, time for dinner.
scoot
This is what we do before dinner.
Thank you for the food Amen.
I'm all done.
Where do you think he picked that up?
I don't--
He was just at my parents' house.
Oh, right.

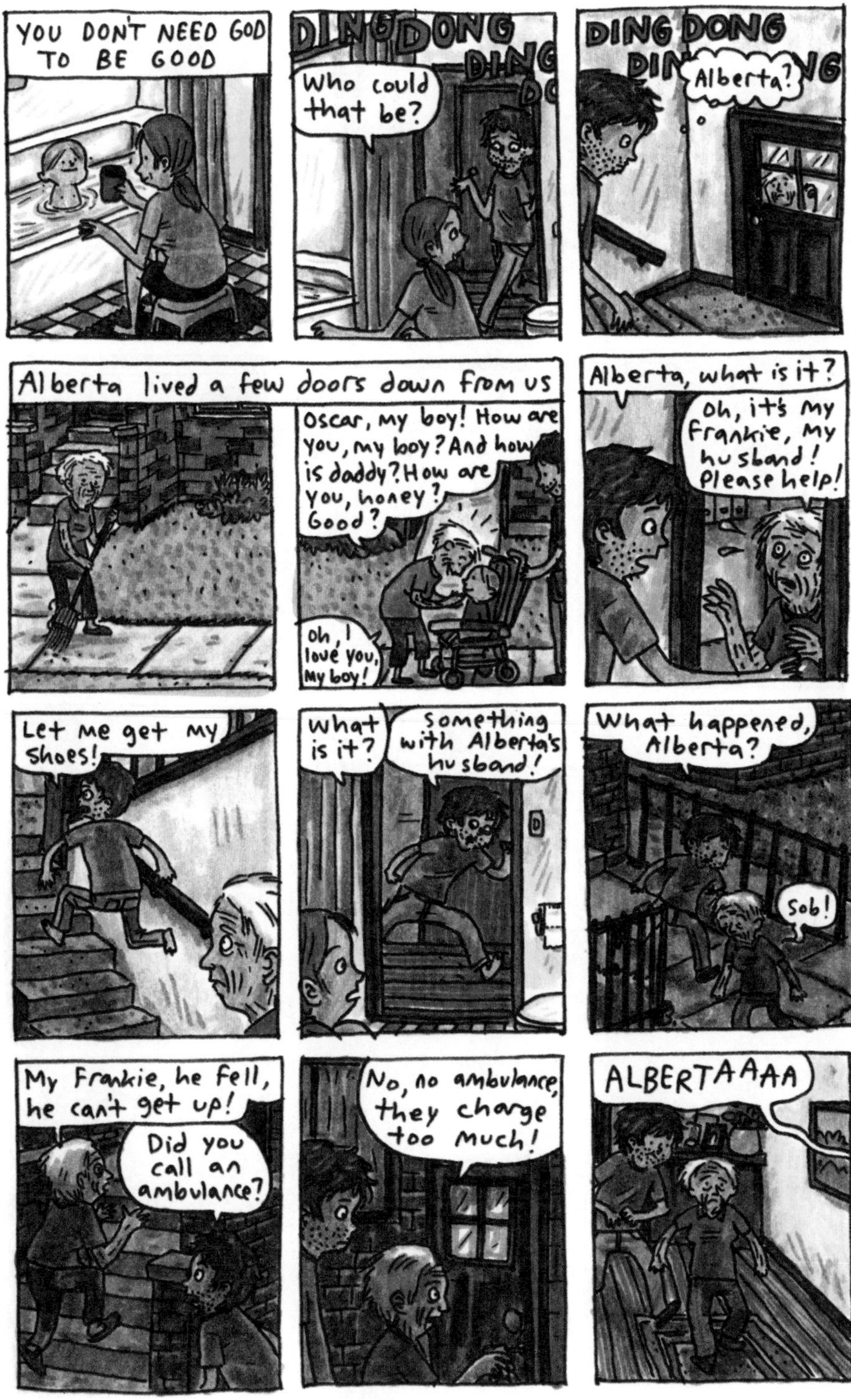
YOU DON'T NEED GOD TO BE GOOD
DING DONG DING DO
Who could that be?
DING DONG DING DONG
Alberta?
Alberta lived a few doors down from us
Oscar, my boy! How are you, my boy? And how is daddy? How are you, honey? Good?
Oh, I love you, my boy!
Alberta, what is it?
Oh, it's my Frankie, my husband! Please help!
Let me get my shoes!
What is it?
Something with Alberta's husband!
What happened, Alberta?
Sob!
My Frankie, he fell, he can't get up!
Did you call an ambulance?
No, no ambulance, they charge too much!
ALBERTAAAA

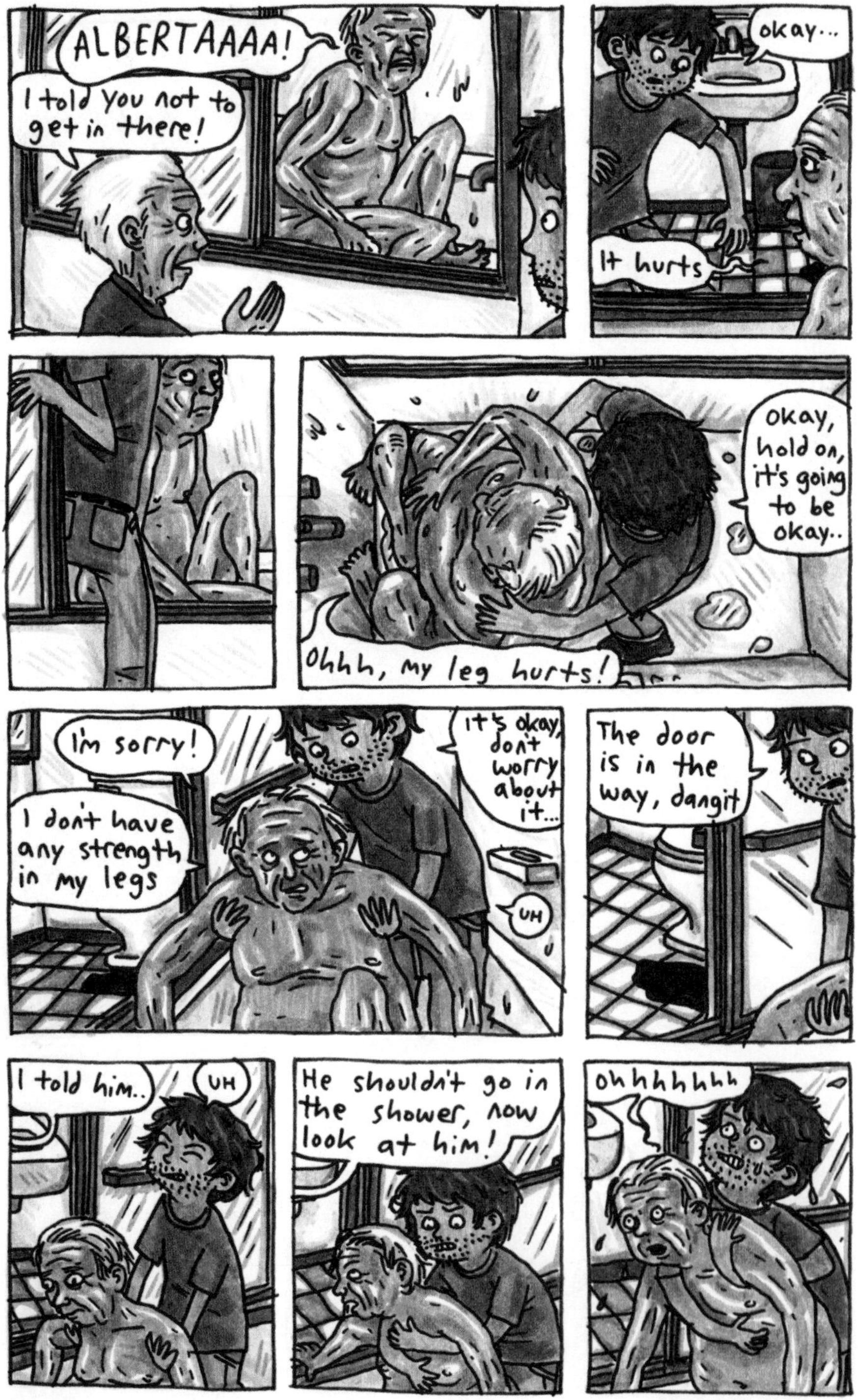
ALBERTAAAA!
I told you not to get in there!
okay...
It hurts
Okay, hold on, it's going to be okay..
Ohhh, my leg hurts!
I'm sorry!
I don't have any strength in my legs
it's okay, don't worry about it...
UH
The door is in the way, dangit
I told him..
UH
He shouldn't go in the shower, now look at him!
ohhhhhhh

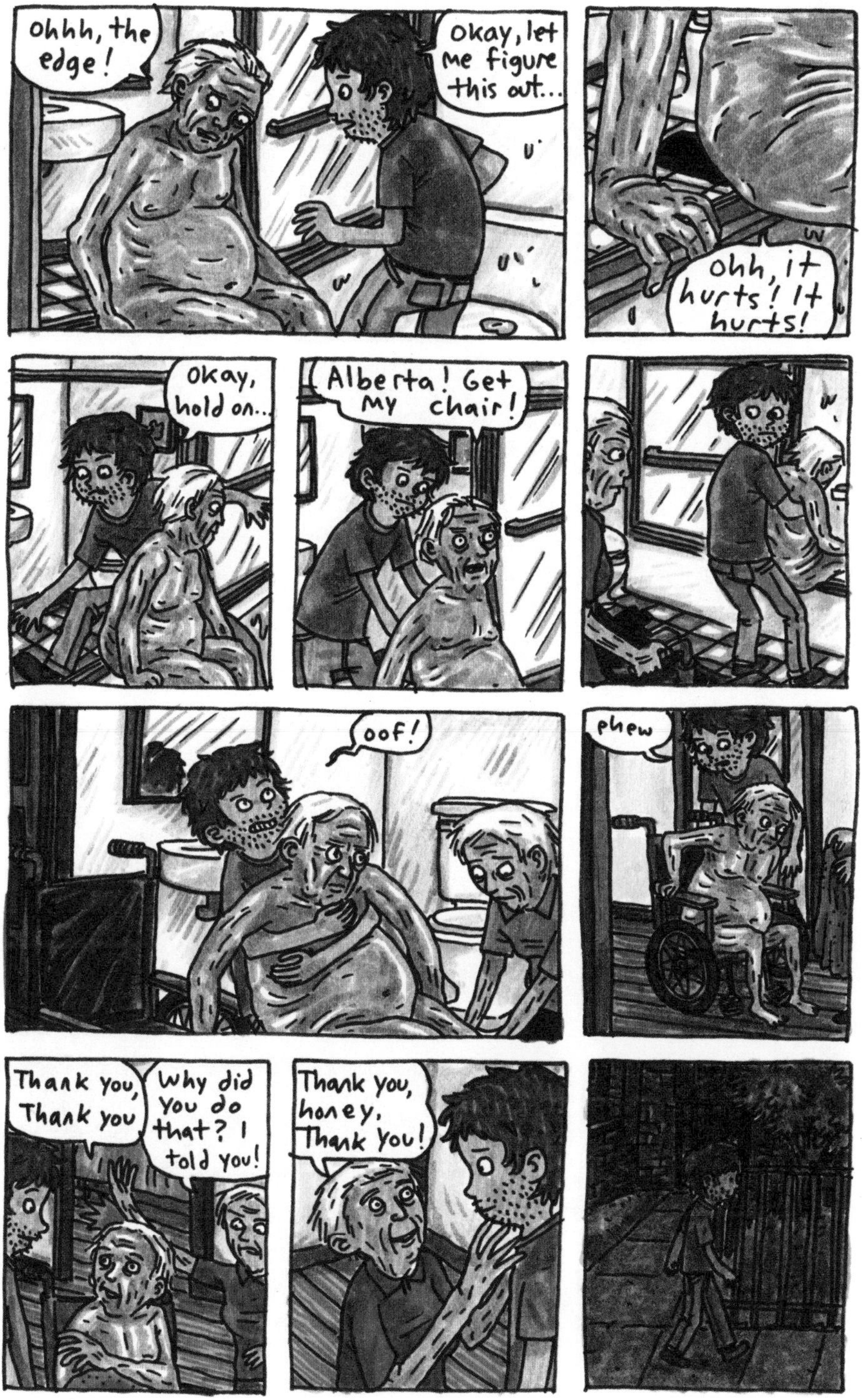
Ohhh, the edge!
Okay, let me figure this out...
Ohh, it hurts! It hurts!
Okay, hold on...
Alberta! Get my chair!
oof!
phew
Thank you, Thank you
Why did you do that? I told you!
Thank you, honey. Thank you!

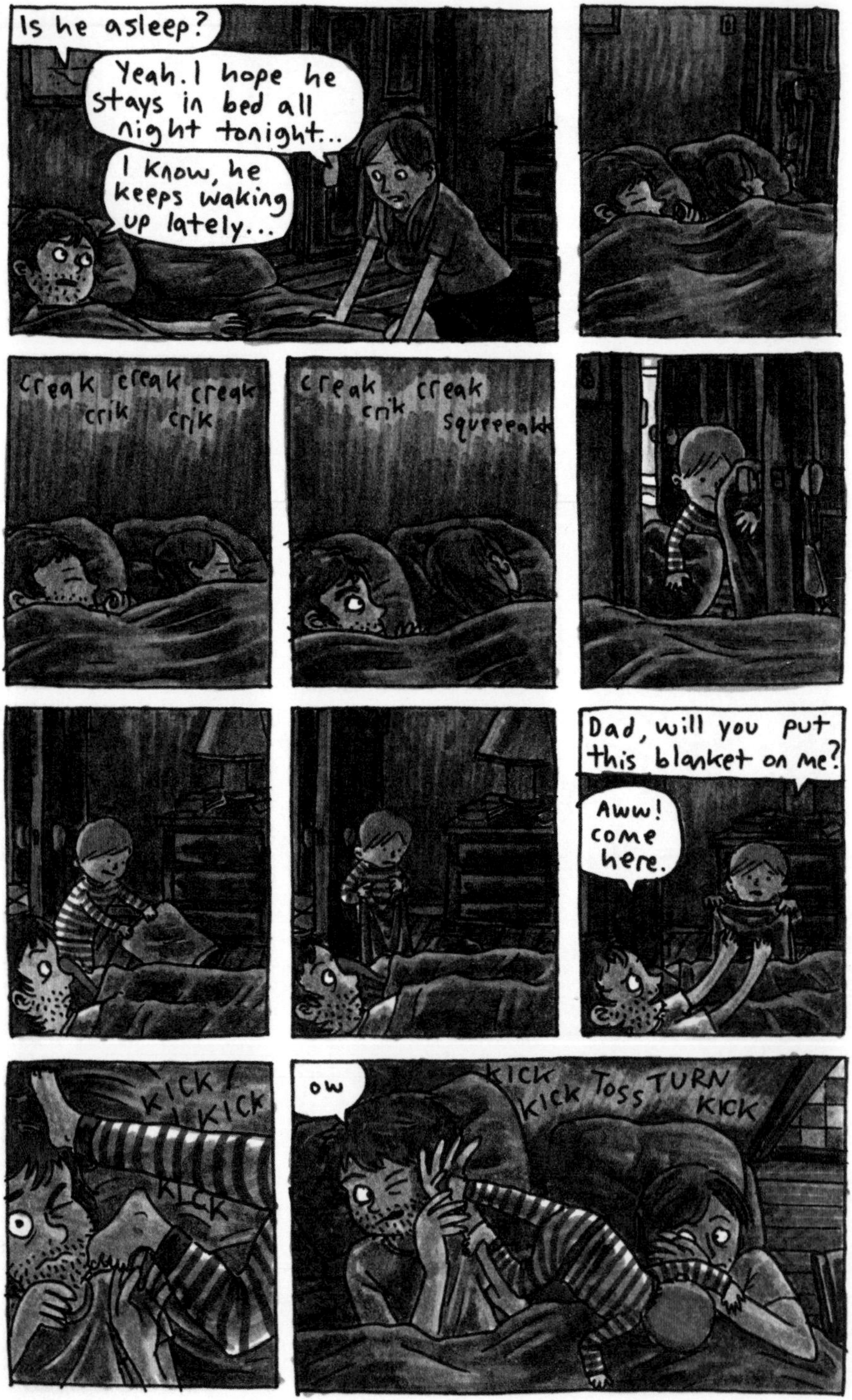
Is he asleep?
Yeah. I hope he stays in bed all night tonight...
I know, he keeps waking up lately...
creak creak creak crik crik
creak crik creak squeeeakk
Dad, will you put this blanket on me?
Aww! come here.
KICK! KICK KICK
KICK
ow
KICK KICK TOSS TURN KICK

BACK TO GRAND RAPIDS

COUGH COUGH

Should we wait for dessert?
COUGH
Yeah, I'm stuffed.

Dad, do you want your surprise?
Okay

Here, Oscar, give these to your Dad.
COUGH

Thanks, Oscar!
COUGH

Here, Dad! Do you know what this is? It's a fossil!
I love it!

He picked it out himself.

One symptom of pulmonary fibrosis is a dry, hacking cough...
Do you know what it is?
An Ammonite?

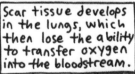

Scar tissue develops in the lungs, which then lose the ability to transfer oxygen into the bloodstream.
COUGH
You're right, Dad!

The standard prognosis is a life expectancy of about five years.

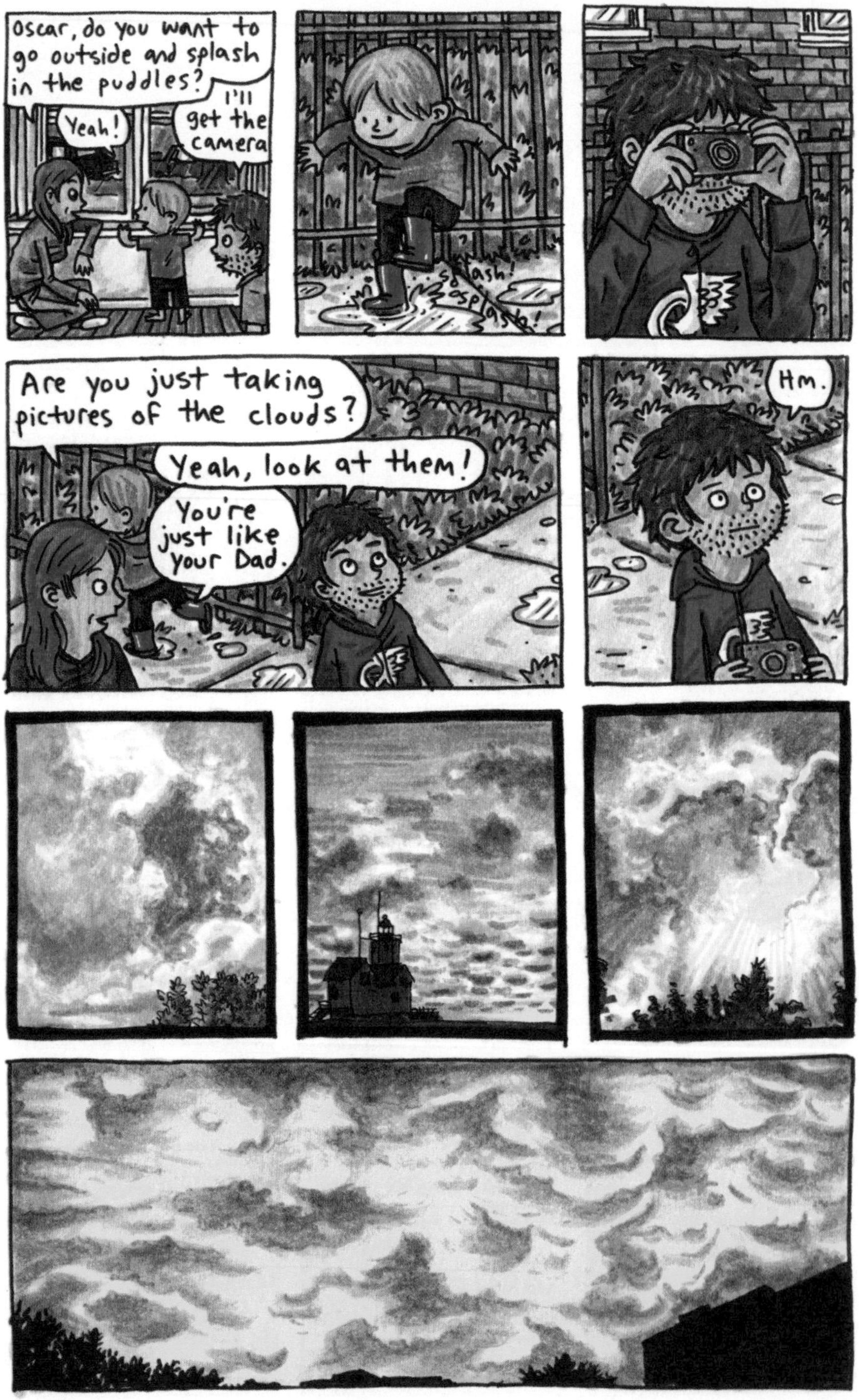
Oscar, do you want to go outside and splash in the puddles?
Yeah!
I'll get the camera
splash!
splash!
splash!
Are you just taking pictures of the clouds?
Yeah, look at them!
You're just like your Dad.
Hm.

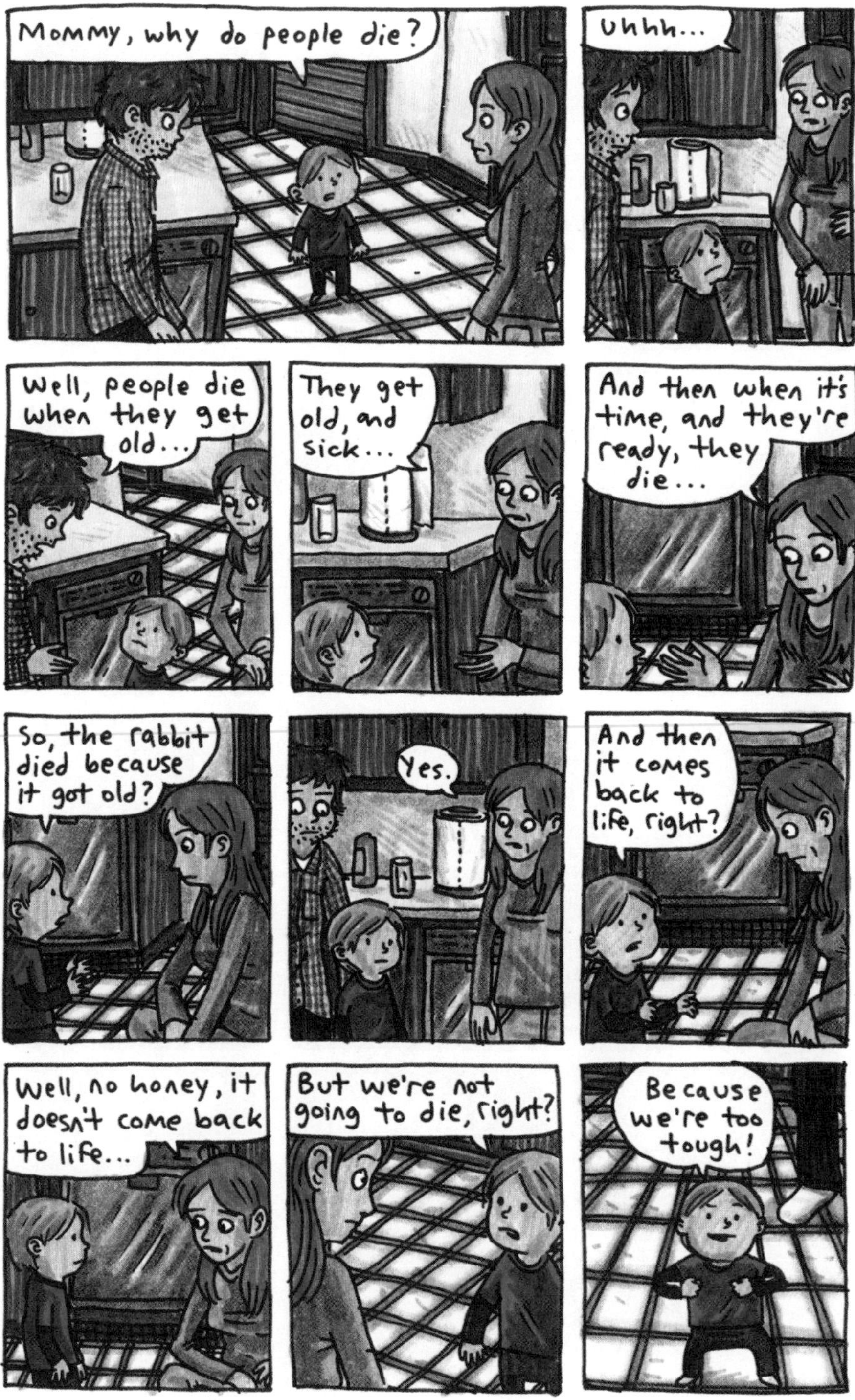
Mommy, why do people die?
Uhhh...
Well, people die when they get old...
They get old, and sick...
And then when it's time, and they're ready, they die...
So, the rabbit died because it got old?
Yes.
And then it comes back to life, right?
Well, no honey, it doesn't come back to life...
But we're not going to die, right?
Because we're too tough!

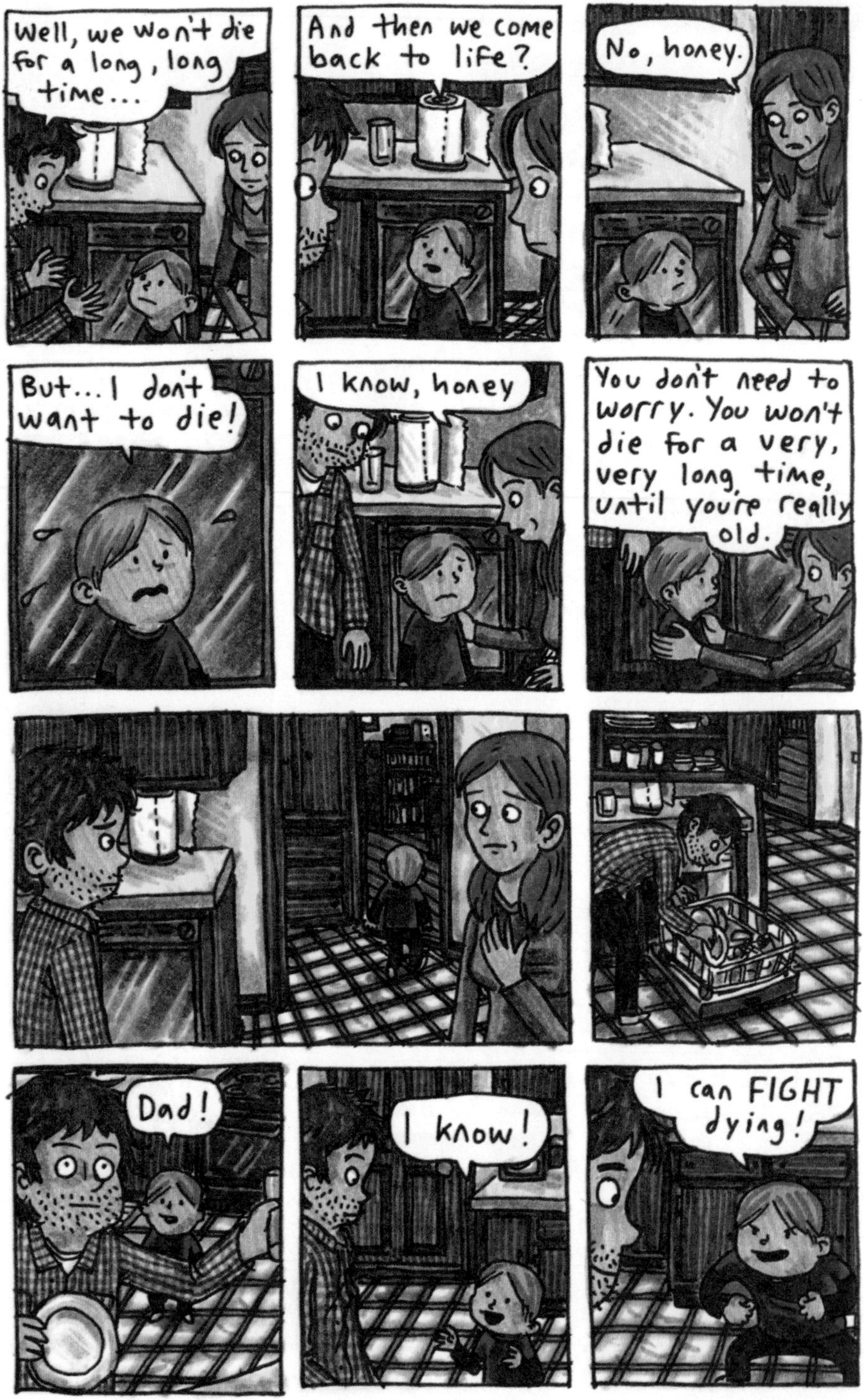

Well, we won't die for a long, long time...
And then we come back to life?
No, honey.
But... I don't want to die!
I know, honey
You don't need to worry. You won't die for a very, very long time, until you're really old.
Dad!
I know!
I can FIGHT dying!

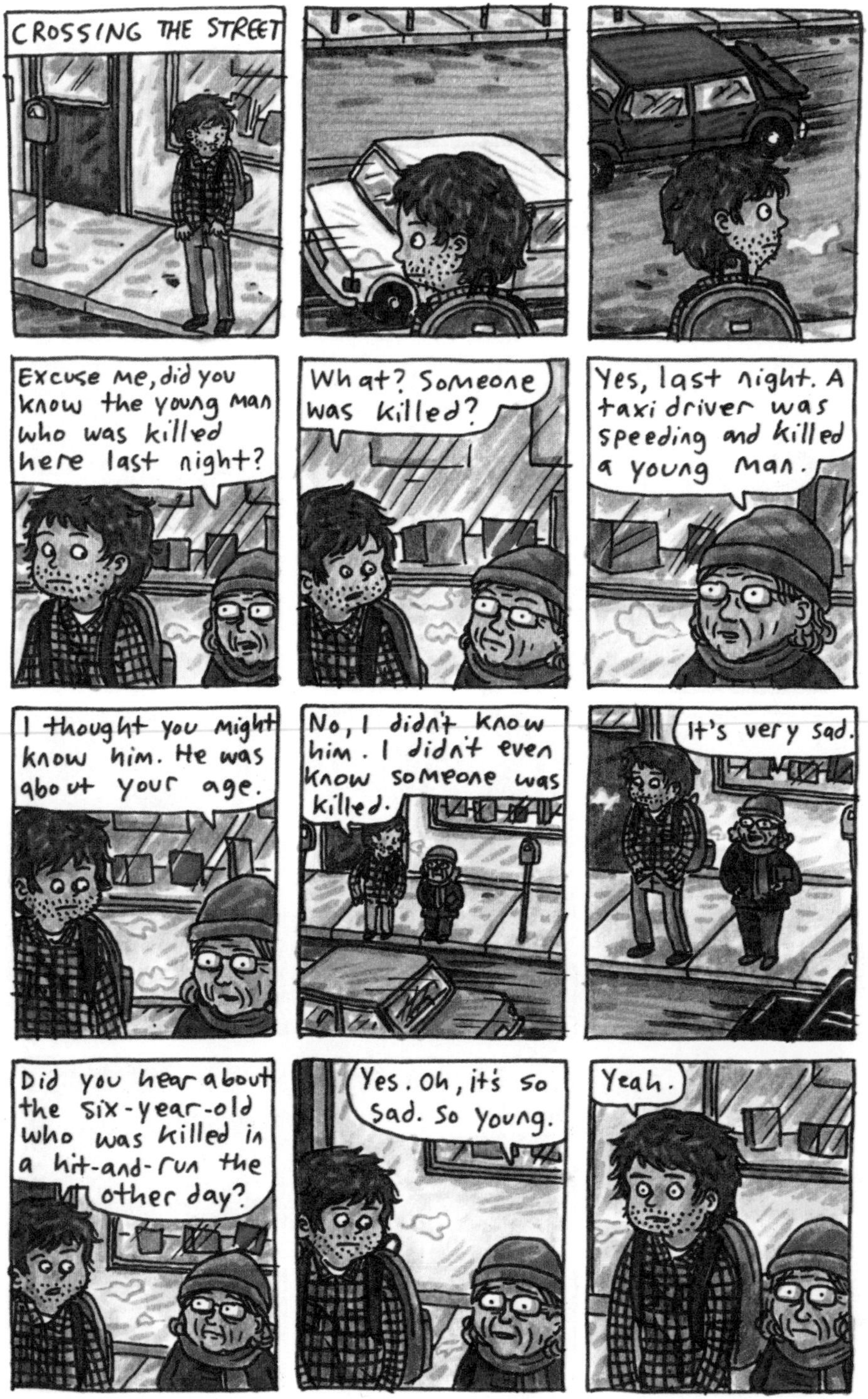
CROSSING THE STREET
Excuse me, did you know the young man who was killed here last night?
What? Someone was killed?
Yes, last night. A taxi driver was speeding and killed a young man.
I thought you might know him. He was about your age.
No, I didn't know him. I didn't even know someone was killed.
It's very sad.
Did you hear about the six-year-old who was killed in a hit-and-run the other day?
Yes. Oh, it's so sad. So young.
Yeah.

Are you a Christian?

Yes.

Oh, bless you, bless you.

I sensed it... oh, you have a gentle- ness about you.

My Dad's a minister.

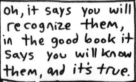

Oh, it says you will recognize them, in the good book it says you will know them, and it's true.

You have a good day.

Oh, you too.

You tell your father he did a good job.

I will.

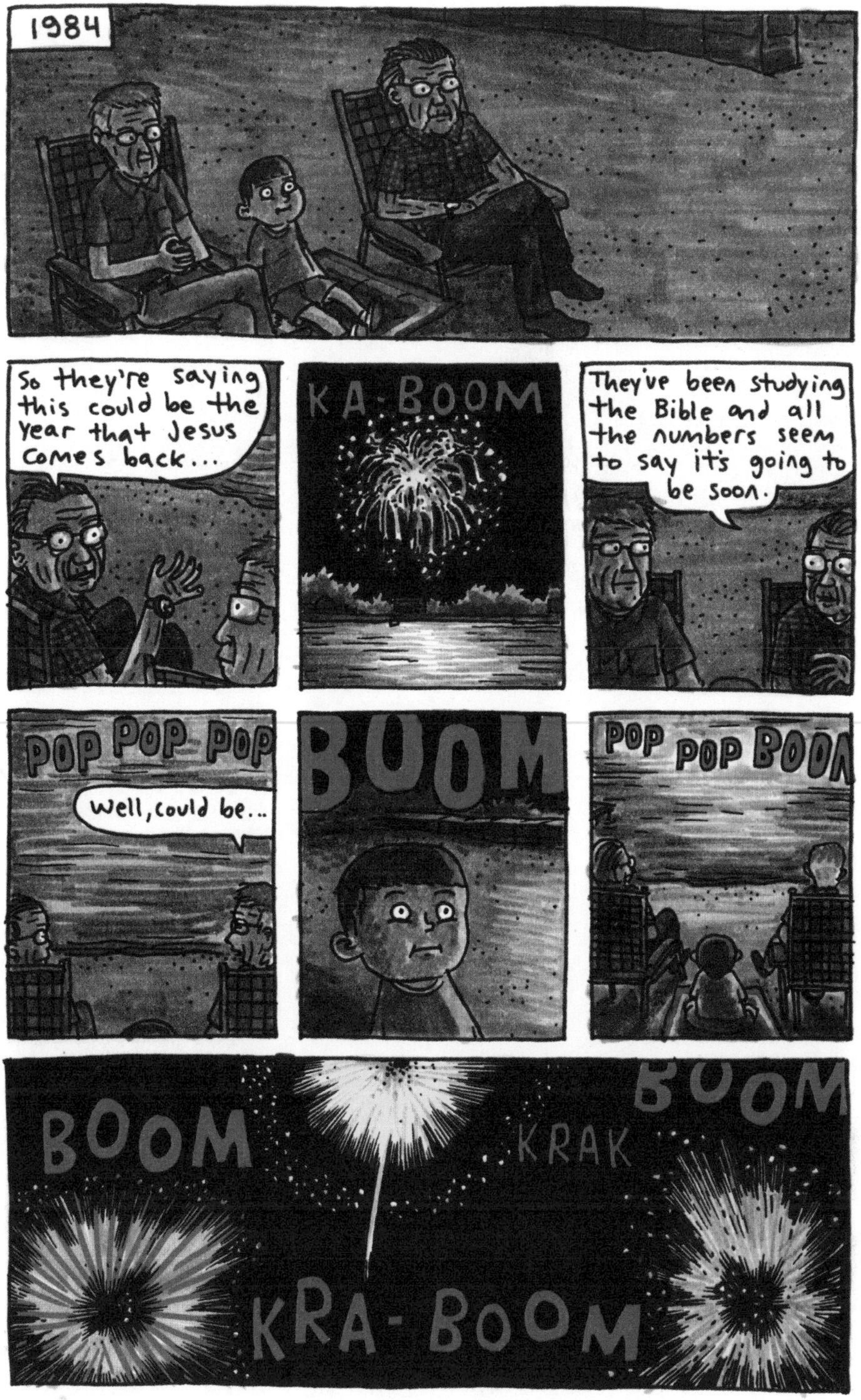
1984
So they're saying this could be the year that Jesus comes back...
KA-BOOM
They've been studying the Bible and all the numbers seem to say it's going to be soon.
POP POP POP
Well, could be...
BOOM
POP POP BOOM
BOOM
KRAK
BOOM
KRA-BOOM

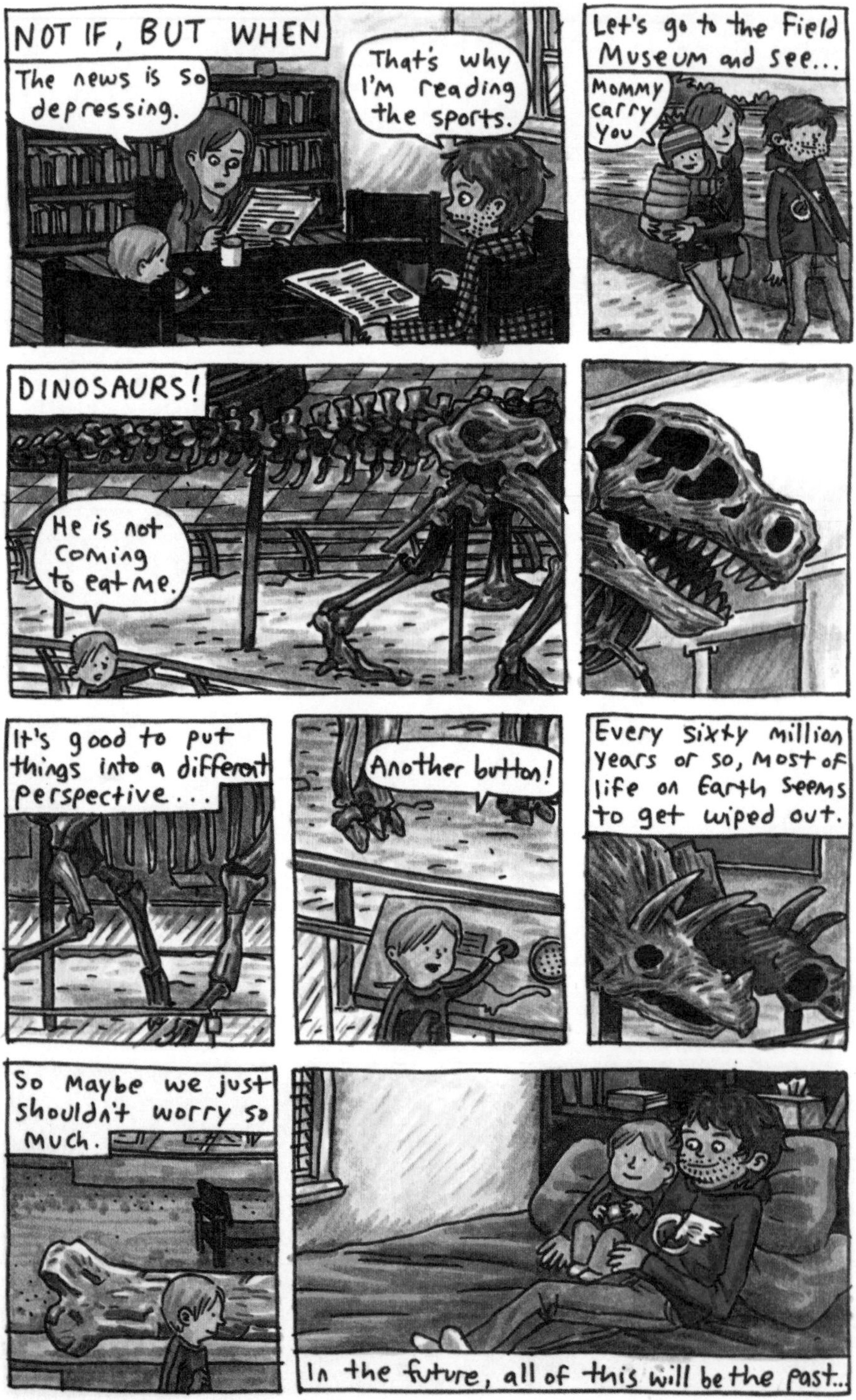
NOT IF, BUT WHEN
The news is so depressing.
That's why I'm reading the sports.
Let's go to the Field Museum and see...
Mommy carry you
DINOSAURS!
He is not coming to eat me.
It's good to put things into a different perspective...
Another button!
Every sixty million years or so, most of life on Earth seems to get wiped out.
So maybe we just shouldn't worry so much.
In the future, all of this will be the past..

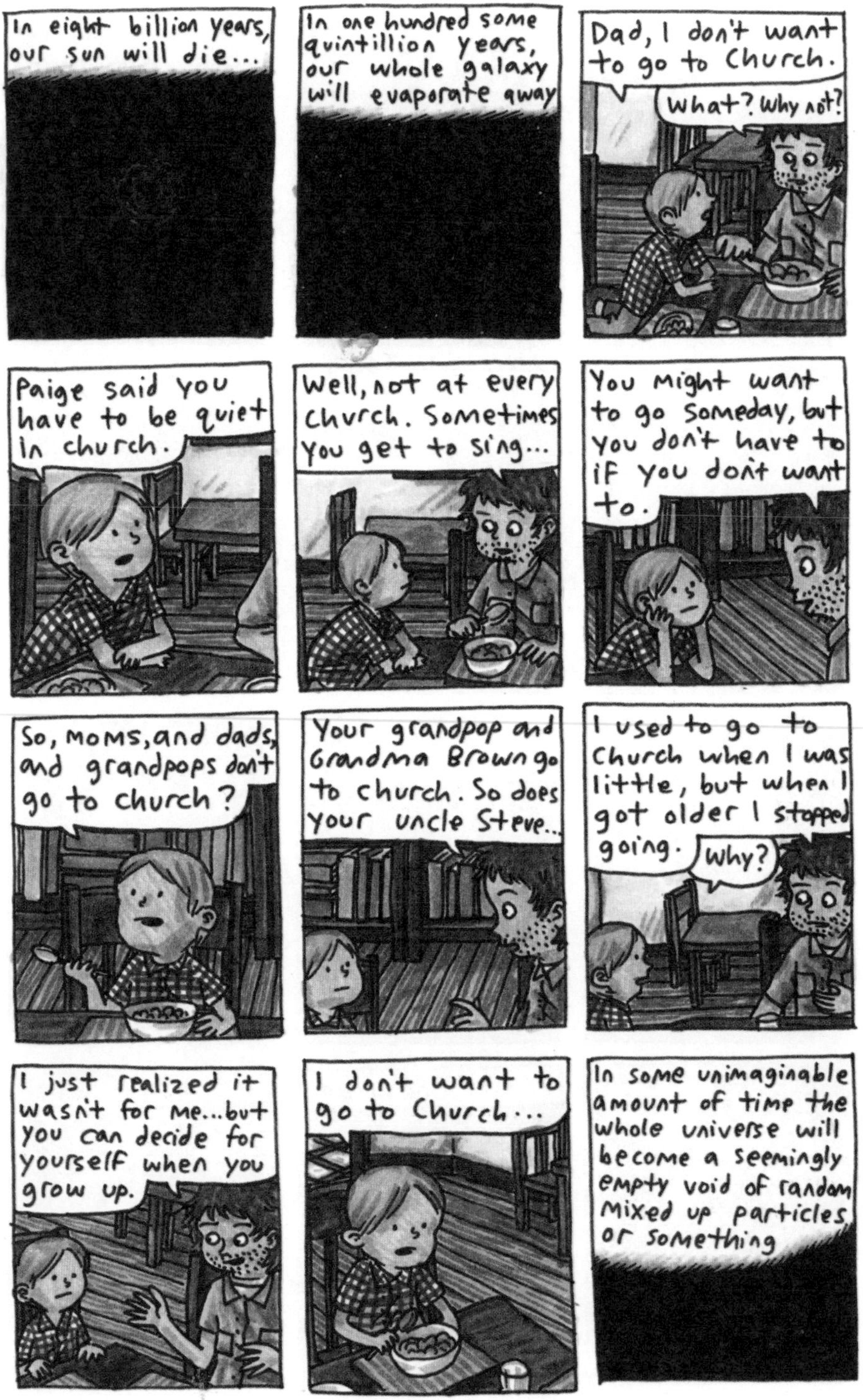
In eight billion years, our sun will die...
In one hundred some quintillion years, our whole galaxy will evaporate away
Dad, I don't want to go to Church.
What? Why not?
Paige said you have to be quiet in church.
Well, not at every church. Sometimes you get to sing...
You might want to go someday, but you don't have to if you don't want to.
So, moms, and dads, and grandpops don't go to church?
Your grandpop and Grandma Brown go to church. So does your uncle Steve...
I used to go to church when I was little, but when I got older I stopped going.
Why?
I just realized it wasn't for me...but you can decide for yourself when you grow up.
I don't want to go to Church...
In some unimaginable amount of time the whole universe will become a seemingly empty void of random mixed up particles or something

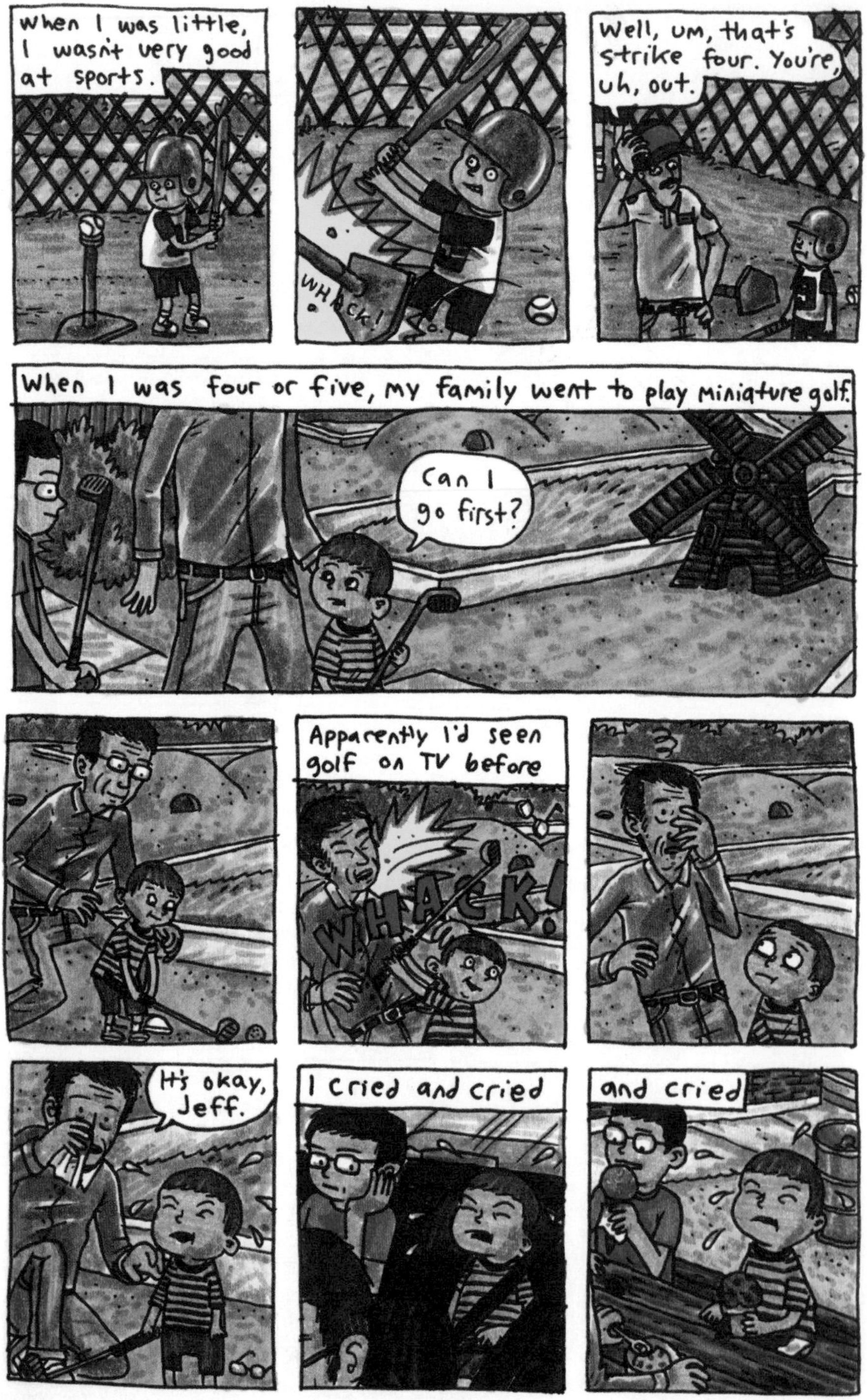

When I was little, I wasn't very good at sports.
WHACK!
Well, um, that's strike four. You're, uh, out.
When I was four or five, my family went to play miniature golf.
Can I go first?
Apparently I'd seen golf on TV before
WHACK!
It's okay, Jeff.
I cried and cried
and cried

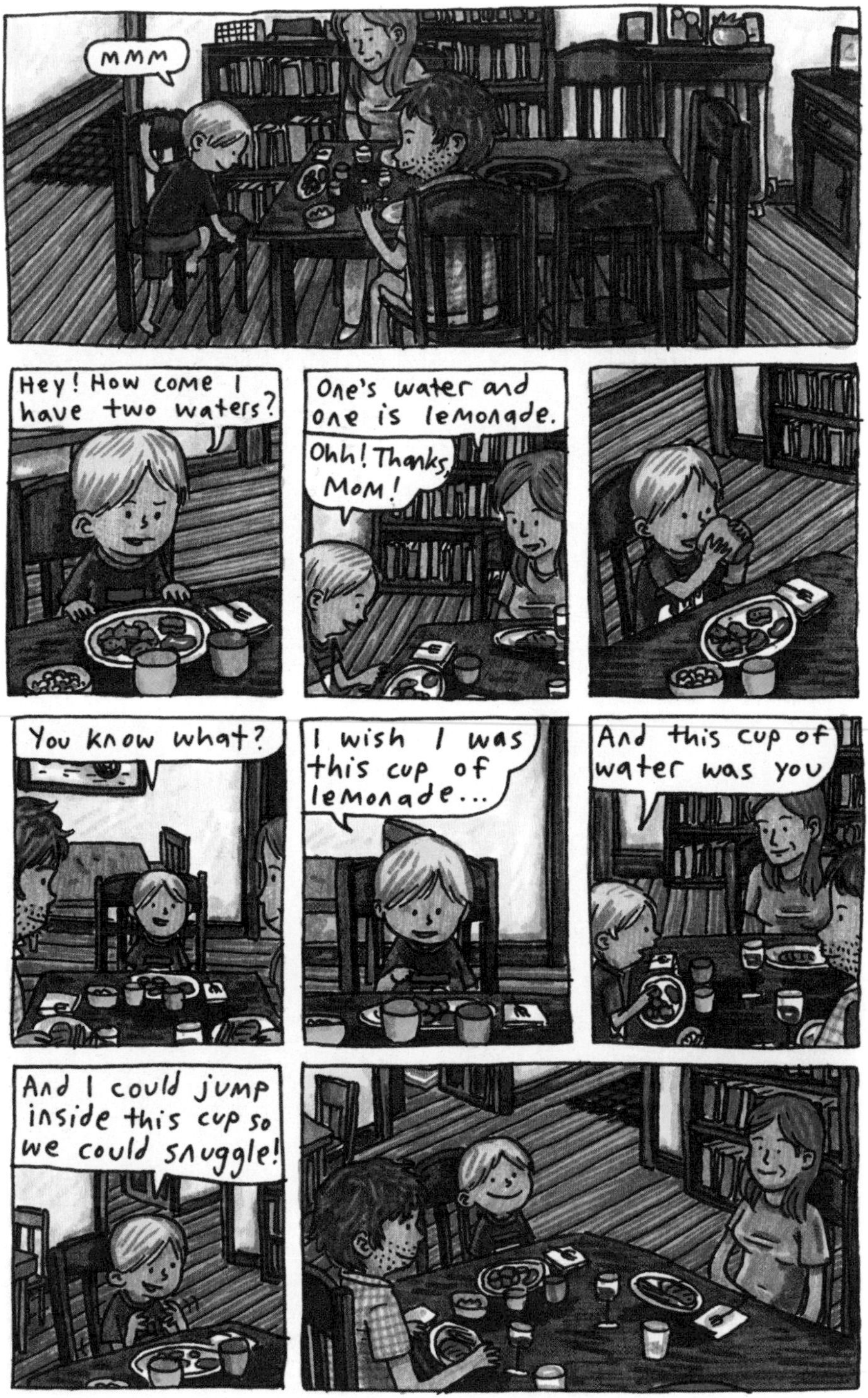
MMM
Hey! How come I have two waters?
One's water and one is lemonade.
Ohh! Thanks, MOM!
You know what?
I wish I was this cup of lemonade...
And this cup of water was you
And I could jump inside this cup so we could snuggle!

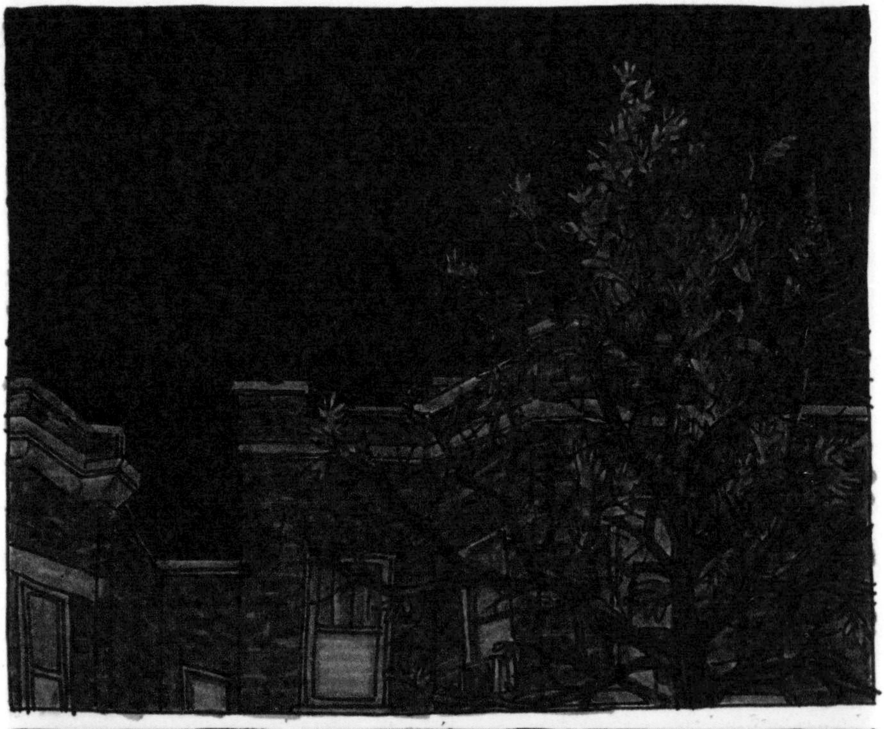

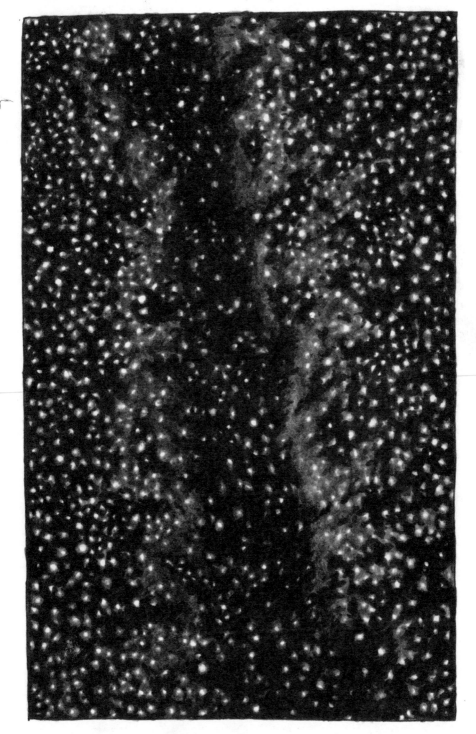

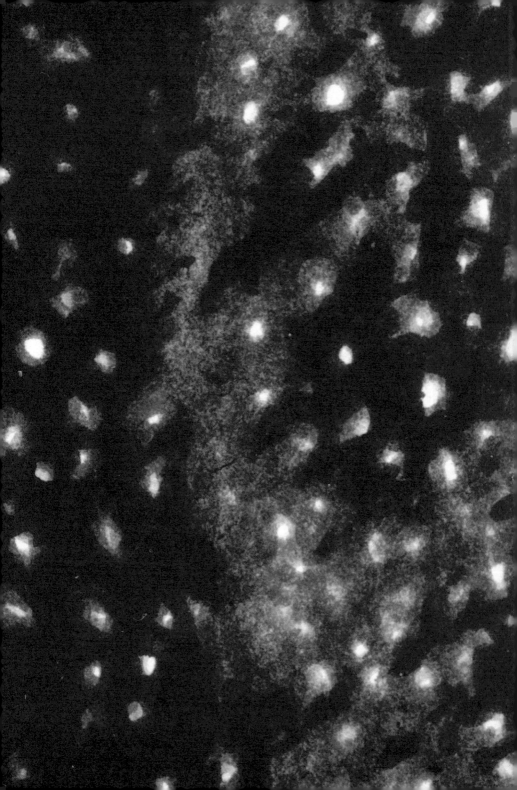

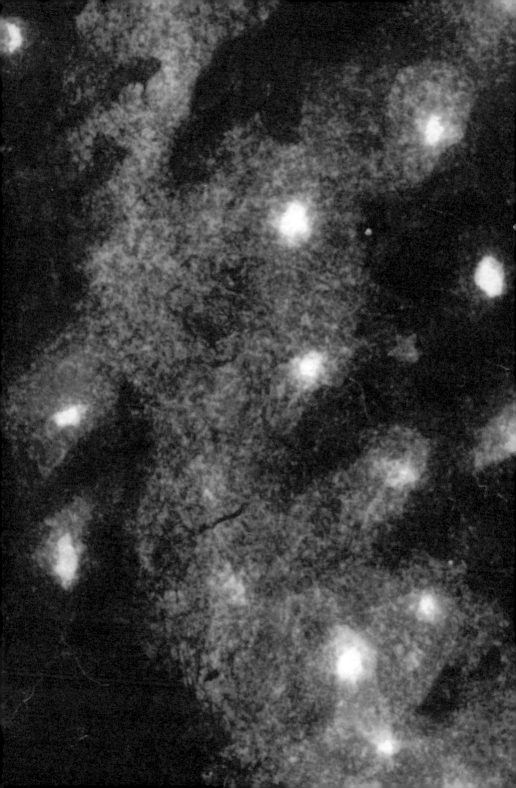

Jeffrey Brown is a cartoonist known alternately for his graphic memoirs (Clumsy, Funny Misshapen Body), humorous parodies (Incredible Change-Bots) and cat books (Cats Are Weird). He has dabbled in film (Save the Date), animation (Death Cab For Cutie: Directions) and radio (This American Life). He currently teaches comics at The School of the Art Institute of Chicago, where he received his MFA in 2002. He lives in Chicago with his wife Jennifer and two sons.

Write to Jeffrey at:
JEFFREYBROWNRQ @ HOTMAIL.COM
P.O.BOX 120 DEERFIELD IL
60015-0120 USA
For more information, visit:
www.jeffreybrowncomics.com
www.jeffreybrowncomics.blogspot.com
www.topshelfcomix.com/jeffreybrown
www.scottedergallery.com

MANY THANKS ARE DUE to a great many people, including: all my family, friends and readers, but especially to: Chris and Brett for publishing this and so much of my work; Doug and Steve for being what brothers should be; Mom and Dad for all the love and support that has helped make me who I am; Jennifer for making me a better person (and making this a better book); and of course, Oscar, for more than words can adequately describe.

ALSO BY JEFFREY BROWN
Jedi Academy
Vader's little Princess
Darth Vader and Son
Incredible Change-Bots Two
Cats Are Weird
Undeleted Scenes
Sulk Vol. 1, 2 & 3
Funny Misshapen Body
Little Things
Incredible Change-Bots
Cat Getting Out of A Bag
Any Easy Intimacy
Bighead
Unlikely
Clumsy

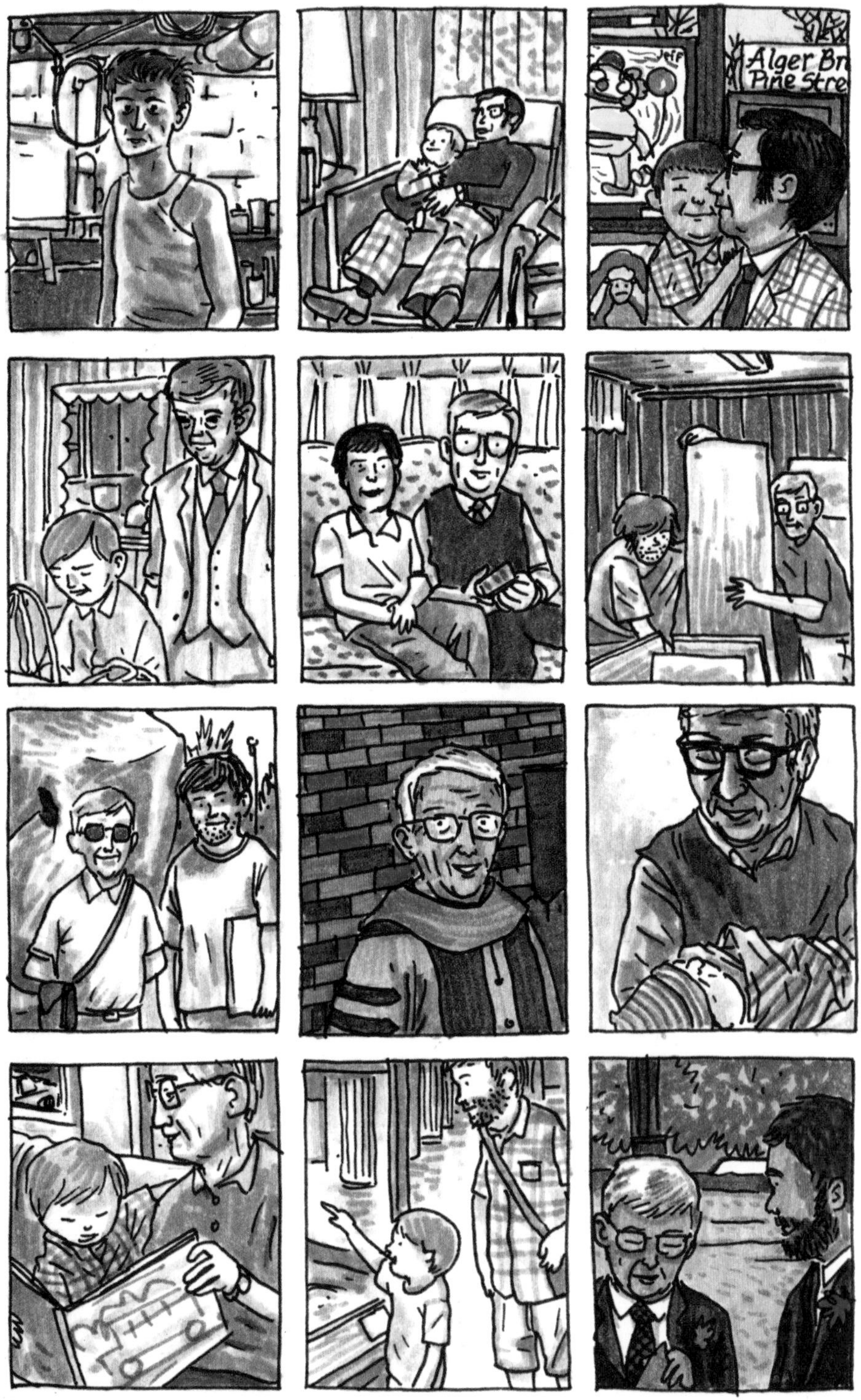
Alger Br
Pine Stre